Dedication

This book is for all those workers who are trying hard to make a difference to the lives of the individuals, families and communities they serve in so many different ways, often with very little thanks. We hope that this book will be useful for you and will make it easier to offer evidence of the impact of what you are doing.

Contents

1   List of tables and figures

Acknowledgements

We are immensely grateful for the support and encouragement of family, friends and colleagues who shared our view that this book was a worthwhile endeavour that could support best practice. In particular, we want to thank Val Chapman who diligently read all our drafts and the many people listed below who have so generously shared their ideas and evaluations with us. Their practical experiences on how to go about outcome evaluation have brought the issues to life for us, and are certain to help those who turn to this book for help in evidencing their results.

Beacon Positive Youth Engagement Peer Support Programme (with its 23 contributing local authorities)

Birmingham Royal Ballet

Catch22

Change Support Difference (CSD) Ltd

Denis Anthony, Professor of Nursing, School of Nursing and Midwifery, De Montfort University

Heywood New Deal for Communities

Kickz

Learning and Skills Council, West Midlands

Leicester College

Lorraine Robinson, Sure Start Children's Centre, Beaumont Leys, Leicester

New Hope Mentoring Programme

Novas Scarman and its workers, Sharon Nembhard and Sherwayne Mitchell

Pip Wilson and Ian Long, for the Blob Tree

Spurgeons Beyond the Horizon

Staffordshire Fire and Rescue Service

St Paul's Community Development Trust, Balsall Heath

The Children's Society Shared Care Solihull Programme

Thilo Boeck, The Centre for Social Action, De Montfort University

Tony Williams, for artwork

VCS Matters

Wildside Activity Centre, Wolverhampton

Women's Aid Leicestershire Ltd

Wirral Council

Youth Action Network and the young researchers on Project Re:action

Youth Affairs Unit, De Montfort University

Introduction

This book is intended as a practical handbook on how to evaluate outcomes and is aimed mainly at managers and practitioners in fieldwork in people-orientated professions. We hope it will find a home on your shelf and be used regularly for reference. Recent emphases in national policy and new commissioning frameworks have created an urgent need for statutory, voluntary and even private sector projects to understand how to evaluate and present the outcomes of their work. This applies in many areas such as supported housing, provision under the Children's Trusts, work with offenders, and health or social regeneration initiatives. Nobody nowadays can avoid the task of performance measurement. This book addresses the practicalities of how to produce evidence of outcomes from interventions in work with people – it is a basic, 'how to' book, primarily aimed at practitioners.

Most of us working in these professions – for example, social work, nursing, youth work, teaching, probation and youth justice, community work, the arts, sports development, mental health, early years services, and so on – came into our jobs because we really wanted to make a difference. We wanted to see positive benefits from our work in the lives of the people we serve. However, we are usually far too busy doing the work to get a proper answer to the question of 'What difference does it all make?' We would rather leave that to policy-makers and researchers, hoping that our instinctive judgements that the work is helping people will be obvious to others as well.

That position, however, leaves us and our projects vulnerable. There has been a sea-change in the demands for evaluation of services. Where once only output measures were required (such as attendance, or the number of patients treated or literacy sessions delivered), now evidence of effectiveness is demanded. The government stress (in both the UK and USA) on 'what works' – on outcomes – is translated into commissioning and monitoring frameworks in plenty. There is little, however, that helps local workers in the average front-line service to go about demonstrating the difference that their work is making to users, and most projects cannot afford external evaluations. Texts on research methods and evaluation do not in the main address this level of practice.

In the coming chapters, we will discuss the reasons for the current focus on outcomes in service planning and social policy. We will explain some of the outcome-driven models of planning in common use, look at how to plan and conduct evaluation at fieldwork level so as to capture the outcomes achieved with service users, and consider the tools available for evaluation and how to use them. This has a direct application to the everyday situation for projects that not only have to deliver services but must also demonstrate their results at the same time. We believe this text can help the many projects that just might not survive without evidence of their outcomes.

This book aims to be practical and accessible. It is based on our experience of providing evaluation and of supporting fieldworkers in undertaking what is necessary themselves. It is liberally illustrated with examples and case studies from real projects in a wide range of fields. In general, we have not given a source for practice examples which are simply drawn from our own experience of helping projects with their evaluations. All other examples provide the reference for the source material.

The book will suggest activities to help you relate the topic to your own work. It includes an explanation of why demonstrating outcomes is so important in the current policy context, a look at the vocabulary of outcome-led planning, and a review of basic approaches to data collection and research methods, the ethics of evaluation, analysis and presentation of reports. It also includes some discussion of the difficulties and dilemmas of the outcome focus.

Primarily, we are writing for the British context. The principles of outcome evaluation are the same, however, wherever you are and can be applied to any social intervention. The emphasis on outcomes is becoming increasingly important as individual countries develop their own service provision and in international work on health, social care, emergency aid or education.

We aim to address the need for evidence of outcomes in a very broad range of services. Terminology can present some difficulties across disciplines but the principles are exactly the same. In different settings the term for the users of the service may vary: pupil, student, patient, client, tenant, member or simply user. We might use several of these terms in an example or just the one most commonly used in the context but we leave it to you to translate across into your own arena.

The book is not intended as an academic text although it may be helpful for students training for the people-orientated professions or undertaking continuing professional development. It does not purport to offer a highly detailed discussion of research methods or compete with established basic texts on methodology, though references are suggested for those who wish to follow up on such aspects.

We hope that you will find some sections of this material that specifically answer the questions you are faced with in evaluating your work. Dip into the material for something you need or work through it systematically. Use it for reference. Make it work for you.

We care about the quality of our services. We, too, want good outcomes for all those who use them. We have encountered scenarios where planners have forgotten that big changes for whole areas or populations are brought about through inch-by-inch progress with individuals and in communities and have therefore demanded instant or unachievable evidence of success from local agencies. We fear there may be an increasing number of situations in the future where projects that do a good job and really do make a difference fail to survive because they cannot produce convincing evidence of their results There are signs that it is already happening. We hope this book will make a contribution to reducing that trend.

CHAPTER 1

Why Should I Want to Evaluate?

If by the time you have taken a good look at this book, you are convinced that time spent evaluating the impact of your work is time well spent, then we will have succeeded in our objective. We want you to see that evaluation of the benefits of your work can pay real dividends for your users and for your organisation, and to have a sense that it is well within your grasp to cope with doing such evaluation. That's the positive outcome we want to see. We believe such evaluation is now a vital ingredient in the recipe for the health and long-term survival of projects working to make a difference in people's lives.

The different reasons for evaluation

Evaluation, however, does take time and trouble. It therefore helps to be clear about why you are investing that effort. An accurate assessment of the reasons for its necessity will sharpen your evaluation design.

There is no harm in recognising that we all have our different agendas about evaluation. Some people feel it is just an extra, to be done if there is time or sufficient resources can be found to bring in external researchers. Others are suspicious or resistant, fearing that it will be imposed from above for dubious reasons. Nobody wants unreasonable or unexpected criticism. However, managers may need to know if the service is running effectively or if what they have commissioned is worthwhile. Frontline staff may want to show that what they do is valuable and deserves recognition.

Throughout this book, we argue that evaluation is absolutely essential. It is an aspect of good practice and effective management. It is so significant that it should be established from Day One of any project and integrated into everything we do. It is an essential part not only of assessing the success of particular projects but also of applying for funding for new ones. Good evaluation design does, however, involve clarifying the reasons for undertaking the work. This is particularly important as a stage before commissioning evaluators.

The most frequent answer to the question of *why* we might evaluate is probably that we want to know if the programme, prevention initiative or treatment 'works' or not. We may need to know for our own internal purposes, to satisfy our funders or to deal with government questions about 'what works'. This is the question of the overall outcome of the programme. The other side of this coin is that, while few of us like having to make changes, we should not be perpetuating programmes that do not have a positive impact.

There are several other good reasons for evaluation. The most obvious one concerns the link to funding. Fundamentally, evaluation shows accountability and can demonstrate that public money has been put to good use. Specific funding regimes will have their own requirements for monitoring and evaluation. It is often a condition of a grant or service-level agreement. The perception that these are hoops that must simply be jumped through is, however, an inadequate understanding of the relationship of evaluation to income generation. None of us should expect to receive resources without accountability. A sound evaluation that shows evidence of the work of your organisation and its positive outcomes in the lives of its users can be a valuable tool in fundraising. The report can be referenced or attached to applications. It can be used as evidence that you have had success in one area and are likely to be effective in another, even where the programme has to break new ground and show innovation. Evaluation can also demonstrate value for money and good management of resources. It can offer measures that show what one scheme costs in comparison to another and how much is achieved for the money spent.

Practice example

Birmingham Royal Ballet is a company with an international reputation for excellence and new creative work. Its charitable education programme benefits more than 9,000 children and young people a year, including those who are unemployed, at risk or who have specific needs. It fosters new talent and offers many an experience of dance for the first time in their lives. Two members of the fundraising department kindly discussed with us their approach to evaluation, and extracts from our interview with them are recorded below.

'Outcomes are relevant to everything we do. For every bit of funding, I create a report that talks about what we've achieved. Hopefully it will make the funders look at anything we send on a future occasion.'

'Most arts organisations inherently feel really uncomfortable with evaluation. They don't instinctively sit down and say "What did we achieve and how do we monitor it?" We feel that people either like it or they don't... But there has been a recent change – people now see they have to do it. Where my view changed was in my last job, where I wanted to fund some tickets to give away [in community arts]. *People wouldn't give us money for that but they would fund outcomes. You can't sit there with a clipboard but you can work with community leaders and ask them what the reactions were – draw us a picture, write a letter. It was surprising what we got... ways of saying thank you. In the space of a year, we went from nowhere to fund about 14,000 tickets over a year and having a network of about 240 community groups... It gave us the evidence base to say to funders that we could demonstrate successful outcomes... People had had a positive experience and said "Yes, I can do that now".'*

'Yeah, that's a learning thing. How do you get over that it should be part of your working practice?... I'm going back to people [major trusts] *every year or so. You need to keep it fresh.'*

'And with sponsors – we talk to them about "What would success mean for you?" And we move on to "How are we going to do that?" We will get articles for you, show your logo, provide tickets for your customers or whatever... And then you go back to say "This is what was achieved". That gives you a framework to say on balance was it worth doing or not. That's not an onerous process.'

'That helps to attract future sponsors... It also helps you to build a relationship. It shows that you care about what the funders want.'

'Funders are now a lot more outcome-focused but the organisations who see the point of evaluation get better results from their fundraising. If you think you've got a god-given right to get funding, you'll suffer. Art for art's sake; art for the sake of culture is not enough now. You've got to have outcomes. Some people will always give. But to increase income exponentially you have to show results. We are further down the road here of saying this is what classical ballet can do for the economy, for communities, for business. We can now say to major donors "why". Why, for instance, should I give money for a new work?... Is it going to make any difference?'

Evaluation may be concerned with service improvement. There may be questions about content or methods of the programme or why 'it works', or perhaps how it compares with other schemes doing the same type of work. Sometimes there is a need to identify how to develop it in the future. There may be questions about whether particular target groups are reached or not, and whether the provision is appropriate for their needs.

In a totally different way, evaluation can improve matters for the service user. It can motivate and help people to see how far they have come, and what they have learned, and to decide their next steps. There are numerous tools that allow the worker to explore how the client feels about their targets, their progress so far and areas they may still need to work on. It can be very encouraging to see that you have progressed and improved from the point where you began. One good outcome has a tendency to generate another. At the end of the process, evaluation can also help to bring closure. It can help the user to say 'Thank you' and 'Goodbye', and value what they have done. It can clarify where they want to go next and turn an ending into the next step in a cycle of progress.

Some evaluations are specifically set up to look at options for the future. The organisation may be at a crossroads about its own direction or may need to make choices about avenues for future funding applications. The evaluation may be examining whether the programme is effective in a way that could be replicated elsewhere. Sometimes the process and systems of the work need to be examined. Teams may not be functioning well or management structures may be overloaded or outdated. Organisational processes are very important and may be the crucial factor that is blocking positive impact.

The intended audience for the report is also a key issue and is a part of understanding the reasons for evaluation. Knowing who will read it will also inform the design. Different audiences will want differing emphases, styles and levels of research. For example, if government is planning to invest millions in, say, parenting programmes or road safety, it will want to see major studies with robust evidence of 'what works'. Schools will usually have a particular interest in their central curriculum and the effect on attainment or behaviour with their age group. In medicine, researchers will be asked to show if a particular treatment or form of support is effective in curing or reducing the condition concerned – and in the case of surgery or drug treatment will need to demonstrate the beneficial results and lack of risk beyond doubt. Partners at local level may be interested in the contribution to National Indicators or specific targets in their Local Area Agreement. At the level of a small project, there may be only say 80 people receiving debt counselling in a year but the counsellors will still need to know whether such intervention is beneficial and will often need to show that evidence in order to raise funds and justify the need for such provision.

Evaluation at different stages of the work

Depending on the purpose for which you are evaluating, the job can be done at different stages. If the task is helping clients to identify their progress or to improve the current provision, then it is best undertaken as you go along in the course of the work. This is often termed 'formative' evaluation. For example, in the education setting, evaluation during a course may reveal that students are not grasping the basic concepts, or that some problem such as lack of study skills or dyslexia is preventing proper completion of the assignments. It is too late to find that out at the stage of final assessment: logic dictates that it must be done while a change in teaching or support can make a difference to the outcome.

Practice example ───────────────────────────────

A scheme for visually impaired children offered Activity Days to enable the children to meet others who shared the same challenges, and to try out new activities. The children's evaluation sheets were glowing. One little girl stood out. Her sheet said that she had not enjoyed it at all. Exploration by the workers showed that she had clearly settled down during the day, made friends and entered into the activities. The key factor was that this child was the only one who had come in her school uniform. The sense of not fitting in had coloured her whole perception of the day. *The publicity and information for these events has been changed to prevent this happening again.*

Probably more evaluation studies take place at the end of a scheme or at the end of each year of a programme. This type of evaluation looks at overall results and effectiveness and is usually termed 'summative' evaluation. Best practice is to complete formative evaluations from time to time as the project progresses as well as a final summative report. Simply focusing on the end results can be counterproductive as we are nearly always dealing with a complex network of organisational needs, human relationships and interactions that may well need adjustment to get the best outcomes for the users of a programme.

In whose interests?

Evaluation is not a neutral activity. The investment of different stakeholders and their responses to it will vary, and it is important to recognise this – if only to help resist manipulation of the evaluation effort. Funding bodies may want to show the success and value of what they have chosen to fund: good outcomes reflect well on a charity or a public body. Managers may need to show that projects are effective for their own profile, status and future career prospects. They may also be keen to develop quality services in their field that will help the clients and prevent social problems. Fieldworkers are likely to be wary of evidence that will affect their own reputation or the way they work but, despite such anxieties, may also genuinely want to see improvement.

For service users, the motivation to take part in evaluation is usually around wanting to help the organisation concerned or to improve the service for themselves or others. A little imagination on the part of the evaluator about what other people might feel about their activity goes a long way to ensuring sensitivity and gaining cooperation. The evaluator needs to try to work out what the agendas of the stakeholders (both service users and commissioners) are likely to be. This will help to ensure that the evaluation is not being influenced to take sides or omit part of the picture. The pressure to emphasise the positives should not be allowed to distort the facts.

When evaluation gets a bad name

Evaluation does not always have a good press and there are certainly plenty of wrong reasons for investing in it. Sometimes, for instance, it is used as a device for ducking management responsibility. The external evaluators are used as a mouthpiece to articulate the reasons for a decision that is seen as being the right course of action but that may be sensitive or unpopular.

Sometimes the management agenda may even be to find evidence that can justify the closing down of a project. Very often evaluation is a last-minute scramble to put together some figures for a funding application or a grant requirement – it is neither thorough nor thoughtful and, in the worst cases, can be contrived evidence. Evaluation can be extremely expensive and sometimes the final report does not address the original questions from the specification. Sometimes particular agencies demand extensive 'bean counting' but cannot or will not explain why they need the information. Despite all the resources absorbed, evaluation can also sometimes produce results that do not stand up to scrutiny, or opaque reports that no one can understand. Jargon and difficult words do not make a poor report any better.

Such bad practice cannot be justified: no more in evaluation than in any other aspect of the work. The fact that poor practice exists is not, however, sufficient justification for avoiding the task of evaluating. If we do not take evaluation seriously we are not doing justice to ourselves, our organisation, our staff or our volunteers. Our users may lose out. We *need* to find out how well we are doing and to ensure that our work and the resources other people have invested in it are paying off in terms of making a positive difference for our clients.

The centrality of outcomes

Whether we like it or not the search for evidence of outcomes is now part and parcel of life in public services. We may feel inclined to argue against it philosophically or because it is just too much bother. We will pick up the question of the pros and cons of the outcome focus again in Chapter 10 but, whatever our views on the subject, collecting evidence of positive outcomes is now essential to survival in the current climate. Credible evidence has to mean more than one or two touching stories. Excellence of organisational procedures is not enough. A belief, however honest, that we are helping people is insufficient. We need factual evidence of the results of the work – not just totals sharing the number of operations performed, the number of young people who attended the summer programme, the number of offenders supervised, and so on.

Outcomes (which will be discussed in much more detail later on) are the answer to the 'So what?' question: 'So what difference does it all make?' Outcomes are the changes or benefits for individuals, families, communities or organisations – whether changes in knowledge, attitudes, practical skills, behaviour, health and wellbeing, or the capacity to cope.

An elderly person whose leg ulcers heal may be better able to get about. A young person may stop 'kicking off' in school and may avoid exclusion. A person who is using heroin may stop or accept less damaging, substitute medication. An adult with a fear of reading may venture into a literacy class and may radically change their life chances by learning to read. A homeless person in a hostel may become better able to cope, progressing to supported housing in a flat on their own. A family may start to exercise more and eat more fruit and vegetables. A community may decide to improve its own environment and take over some disused land for an allotment, enabling many families to grow their own fruit and vegetables and making the place look more attractive into the bargain. All these scenarios show positive outcomes.

Such small changes can snowball. Tiny changes add up. The efforts to change made by individuals and all the partners supporting them can eventually make a difference in the population as a whole. Measures such as crime rates, mortality from coronary heart disease, or unemployment begin to improve. The smallest projects, and even individual workers, can and do contribute to this cumulative effect but they will always be vulnerable if they cannot articulate the outcomes they achieve and how these contribute to the whole picture.

Few areas of service provision are now unaffected by the drive for better outcomes. Perhaps the best known are the changes brought about by the Every Child Matters report (DfES 2003). This seminal document followed the case of Victoria Climbié, who died in February 2000 at the age of eight after suffering appalling torture at the hands of her guardians. At their trial for her murder, the judge called the child protection authorities 'blindingly incompetent' but this was not the first case of its kind nor, by a long way, has it proved to be the last in the series of horrific child-abuse cases. The report was intended to address the means of preventing such cases happening in future and of building better outcomes for children. It articulated five key outcomes, which have shaped all subsequent planning and provision in services for children and young people in Britain. These are the need for children to:

- Be healthy
- Stay safe
- Enjoy and achieve
- Make a positive contribution
- Achieve economic wellbeing.

It is impossible to argue against such aims. They seem self-evidently desirable. What is significant about *Every Child Matters* in this context is not the broad outcomes set out but the way in which they have subsequently been broken down into detailed targets to inform all the planning of services for children and young people in England. Local authorities and their partners such as the health services or the police now work together in 'children's trusts' or 'children and young people's strategic partnerships' to identify local need, plan provision and commission services. The use of resources is informed by the drive to improve performance on the five key outcomes. Any organisation that cannot show how its work contributes to those outcomes is unlikely to receive public funds for work with children and young people.

The government's Commissioning Framework guides all such planning. It emphasises the need to start not with the pattern of current provision but with the desired outcomes and the question of which interventions are most likely to produce them. It recommends a detailed study of local needs amongst children and young people, followed by the commissioning of services to meet them. At the end of the cycle the monitoring and review processes kick in. Every service provider will need to show from their evaluation evidence how effectively they contributed to achieving the relevant outcomes. The planning cycle recommended in that framework (HM Government 2006) is shown diagrammatically at Figure 1.1.

Most other services now show similar trends: they are becoming driven by outcomes and demanding that service providers show evidence of their contributions to the chosen outcomes. The majority of trusts, lottery funds

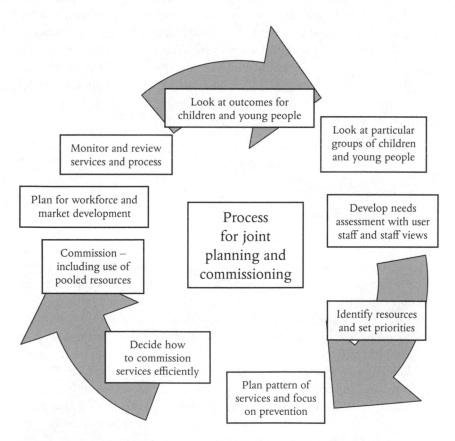

FIGURE 1.1: THE COMMISSIONING FRAMEWORK FOR PLANNING CHILDREN'S AND YOUNG PEOPLE'S SERVICES

and charities are also following suit. Some services are required to work to quality standards in their practice but these standards are also designed ultimately to increase positive results.

To take another example, 'Supporting People' is the government funding stream for housing support for vulnerable groups. It helps over a million such people to live independently in their own homes or within supported accommodation. In 2007, Supporting People launched its Outcome Framework, which is based on the five high level outcomes of *Every Child Matters* and is then broken down into specific Supporting People 'outcome indicators'. For short-term clients, for instance, under the heading of 'Achieving Economic Wellbeing', providers are asked to monitor whether a client is in need of maximising their income, receiving their correct benefits and reducing their debts, and if so, whether or not those outcomes were achieved.

Supporting People has introduced an online outcome-monitoring system so that the data can be gathered nationally to demonstrate the financial and individual benefits of the programme. At the same time, the programme recognises that the choice of the detailed outcomes has to be to some extent a compromise and that other assessments may also be necessary and valid.

> *The development of the detailed indicators did involve considerable debate about the difference between harder, more measurable outcomes and softer outcomes that better represent the distance travelled by service users... The distance travelled approach is clearly very relevant at an individual service user level and can provide a valuable tool within support planning processes. The ability of both providers and service users to demonstrate the achievements... via the distance travelled approach should not be underestimated. (Centre for Housing Research 2007, p.5)*

In primary health care, there is also a Quality Outcome Framework, which looks to improve outcomes on a number of health problems (Department of Health 2004). For a specific disease category, clinical indicators are set out for monitoring. There are, for example, 12 indicators for the management of coronary heart disease by General Practitioners, based on medical evidence that carrying out such management and treatment will contribute to reducing mortality and increasing life expectancy. There are also indicators on record-keeping, practice management and patient-satisfaction surveys. The results are related to financial incentives for individual practices. The Department of Health has recently consulted about the potential for allowing a degree of local flexibility and for choosing new indicators, and is now embarking on a new system for their development (Department of Health 2009).

There are outcome targets now in nearly every field of public services. They are currently prioritised and made more coherent in a set of 198 National Indicators to which local authorities and their partners must work (Department for Communities and Local Government 2009). The themes touch on economic activity, the environment, health, education, housing, community safety and criminal justice. Most of these indicators are measures of the achievement of outcomes. For example, the following outcomes are regarded as desirable targets for local work:

- a reduction in the re-offending of young offenders
- a reduction in the number of people killed or seriously injured in road traffic accidents
- a reduction in the proportion of overweight and obese children in the population
- an increase in the achievement of pupils in school at level 4 or above in both English and Maths at Key Stage 2
- an increase in the expectancy of life to be spent in good health
- an increase in the number of adults with learning disabilities living in settled accommodation.

At present the local partners also set some of their own outcome targets, which are embodied in Local Area Agreements.

Activity

It is essential that you can link your work to its intended outcomes. It may seem incredible but there are many workers who do not even know what outcomes they are supposed to achieve! In some cases, their managers know full well but do not feel it is necessary to pass this on to front-line staff.

- Do you know which agency funds your work?
- Do you know if outcomes are set for this funding and, if so, what they are?
- Can you identify how the difference you make in your own work contributes to those outcomes as a whole?

If you cannot answer these questions positively, you need to start finding out these details so that you are better prepared for the task of evaluating outcomes.

This emphasis on outcomes is not solely a British phenomenon: indeed, it probably had its origins in the social policies of the United States that made a point of seeking evidence of 'what works' in order to plan major programmes of intervention. An illustration from the world of education and services to children is the 'No Child Left Behind Act 2001', which was signed into law in the United States in 2002 (US Department of Education 2001). This Act made each state responsible for setting targets aimed at improving educational outcomes. Students at all levels are tested on basic skills and more general indicators are also set for other areas such as health and wellbeing. The results are monitored locally and nationally. Schools can be penalised or identified for improvement if their outcomes do not reach the required standards.

Turning to the international field, UNICEF is a leading children's organisation reaching into more than 150 countries. It aims to 'work with local communities, organisations and governments to make a lasting difference to children's lives'. It, too, has programmes of monitoring and evaluation and specifically shows how the aims of the United Convention on the Rights of the Child are all relevant to the five Outcomes of *Every Child Matters* (UNICEF 2006). Parallel examples of such policies which emphasise the drive for outcomes can also be found, both in Britain and in other countries, in criminal justice, health or economic regeneration.

All this may sound rather dry and dusty: it seems to belong to a world of bureaucracy. Nonetheless, none of us in the helping professions can afford to ignore it. In any field of work, the outcomes specified in the policies shape the provision that is commissioned and paid for. Every project should be able to locate its work as contributing somewhere to one or more of these outcomes and, in a direct relationship to the theme of this book, it should be able to show evidence of that contribution. The individual outcomes required may change: the systems for monitoring them will undoubtedly change over time in different fields. The drive for outcomes is, however, highly unlikely to go away. We are already witnessing local projects failing to secure continued funding, not because they are known to be doing poor quality work but because they have failed to show evidence of their outcomes. It's time to get our heads round outcome evaluation!

CHAPTER 2

Why is Outcome Evaluation so Crucial?

Survival in the current climate

This chapter develops the arguments from Chapter 1 about the centrality of outcomes and the need to evidence them in the current climate. This has become an essential skill simply for survival in the modern context. Very few services dealing with people now have secure permanent funding. Even schools and hospitals are engaged in battles for funding and what amounts to enforced entrepreneurialism in order to stay in the game. Services can be passed like parcels from one contractor to another as tenders are won and lost and under 'transfers of undertakings' the staff can be moved forwards and backwards between employers. Most organisations will have at least some short-term funding or will be affected by the emerging commissioning process. Even the statutory services provided by law and normally run by local authorities or central government agencies are entering this arena as it is clearly inequitable if the processes of scrutiny apply only to the voluntary or private sector. We are already familiar with situations where private sector companies are running schools, hospitals and prisons, and the trend to diversification is not likely to be halted.

The issue of outcomes does place the competing organisations on a somewhat more even footing. Nobody who fails to produce good results is likely to survive for long when evidence of outcomes is persistently demanded. Organisations with no track record and no evidence at all of previous effective work are going to find it very hard to get a foot on the ladder. Being able to show evidence of the impact of your work on the people you serve becomes absolutely critical. Evaluation is imperative.

If you are mainly interested in the practical questions of how to start on your evaluation, you may wish to move on to the next chapter. However, if your role involves applying for funding or dealing with commissioners, then this chapter provides more background to the changes that are hitting you on a daily basis, and may equip you to cope with them more effectively.

The policy context

Over approximately the past thirty years in Britain, there have been profound changes in the way public services are managed – changes that have brought us to the present emphasis on outcomes and on commissioning of services. 'Welfare states' and 'welfare systems' can be found in numerous forms and although they are generally seen as a twentieth-century phenomenon, forms of welfare provision for the needy can be traced back thousands of years. In Britain, the National Insurance contribution to pay for unemployment and health benefits was introduced in 1911, and the steady growth of the welfare system followed after World War II. At that time, the purist vision was of the State providing a safety net for everybody, with guaranteed minimum standards and the best possible services. To a greater or lesser extent, there are similar systems in most countries that have a developed economy able to support them, though there are variations in policy, how services are organised, paid for and run, and in the resulting outcomes (Spicker 2008).

The early aspirations and assumptions of welfare development have not, however, been straightforwardly delivered. When the welfare state was first established, most people undoubtedly enjoyed improved standards of housing and other basic entitlements: indeed most of us still benefit from the welfare system in some way today. Welfare provision is not, however, static and problems in its delivery soon began to emerge. The bill for welfare benefits and pensions is now breathtaking; the economy and the taxes it can generate are no longer able to sustain constantly rising costs and expectations. In the face of these dilemmas, succeeding governments have made changes to the way in which welfare provision is planned and delivered, with some blurring of old political lines. The Thatcher Government (1979–1990) introduced privatisation and greater competition so that the private and voluntary sectors could bid for service contracts – in part to ensure that the profits could be accessed by the private sector but also in the belief that efficiency and value for money could be improved. The succeeding Labour Government replaced 'compulsory competitive tendering' with the gradual move to the commissioning process but did not remove the notion of competition or return to monolithic state provision (Field 1999). There was an increasing emphasis on the way in which the framing of the call for services through tenders or commissioning could shape the nature of the provision and drive service improvement. Voluntary organisations in particular saw a significant shift from grant-giving regimes, where they had proposed the nature of provision they could offer and requested assistance to deliver it, often for many years at a time. They now moved into the commissioning and tendering scenario where local or central government would specify the service required and the voluntary organisation would be part of a competitive process to win the contract to deliver it.

We can therefore see that as the costs of the welfare system multiplied, greater competition was introduced, closely followed by the move to commissioning. The final link we want to trace in the development of welfare provision is to the use of the outcomes in planning and monitoring. On the one hand, provision cannot sit still: the expectations for constant improvement create real political pressures. On the other, with the welfare system creaking on its hinges, governments cannot afford multi-million pound investments in programmes that do not produce the intended changes. The design and evaluation of programmes to deliver outcomes has moved centre stage. It can be found in almost all policy documents and on virtually any government website in the form of phrases about 'what works' and 'evidence-based practice' that we explained in Chapter 1.

One clear example of this shift to the outcome emphasis is the latest development in the way in which the concept of 'welfare' is framed. The present Labour administration announced a programme of welfare reform in 2008. Designed to tilt the balance back from rights to responsibilities, it is focused on 'deepening and widening the obligation to work' and requiring virtually all those without work to take up the support designed to enable them to find work (Department for Work and Pensions 2008a).

Following through the notion of moving people from benefits into work, the Department of Work and Pensions has now published its own commissioning strategy. This has all the hallmarks of the shifts on welfare thinking that take us, as the Ministerial introduction puts it, 'away from a mindset of top-down control into a world where we devolve initiative and innovation' (Department for Work and Pensions 2008b). The strategy outlines how the Department will buy services from providers of training and other services for those who are unemployed. Very large contracts will be let in the welfare-to-work market to top-tier providers from the public, private or voluntary sectors, who may in turn subcontract to others. The

Department's role will be not only to commission and create a 'robust supply chain' but also to 'drive up performance'.

The ultimate vision is one proposed by David Freud, who worked as an independent adviser to the Labour government but has since joined the Conservative Party as a frontbench spokesperson. His plan speaks of a simplified benefit system and a reduction in benefit costs for those who enter or re-enter the labour market that will balance the cost of the training and support provided (Freud 2007). The significant point here for our purposes is that contracts can be terminated or adjusted in line with performance and that the Department intends to 'trial different models of outcome payments' (Department for Work and Pensions 2008b, p.22), rewarding those providers who succeed in helping people to progress into jobs and improve their skills and earnings. This approach may well mellow in the face of the real difficulties of finding work in a deepening recession but it shows quite clearly that the philosophy of outcomes is embraced across all shades of the political spectrum. Whatever happens there is little doubt that this will prove to be another example of where the targets set for performance affect the nature of the work and the relationship between the professional and their clients.

The drive for outcomes is less stark in some services than in the world of welfare-to-work but it can usually be traced in the background to major programmes of provision. Following the Green Paper 'Youth Matters' and the government's ten-year strategy for positive activities, the Youth Service and other services for young people, for instance, have been funded in recent years to increase constructive voluntary activities outside of school (Department for Education and Skills 2005; HM Treasury and DCSF 2007). Local authorities have a legal duty to secure a menu of attractive provision and publicise this to young people and their families. The programme has now become known as Positive Activities for Young People.

In a recent speech to the Local Government Association, the Minister for Children and Young People, Beverley Hughes, argued that 'having safe, fun, engaging things for young people to do in their communities is not just nice to have – not an optional extra – but essential for their development', helping to build foundations for good future outcomes (Hughes 2009). She suggested that the evidence indicated that such activities stimulated cognitive development, developed other skills such as problem-solving and teamwork, and improved the ability to be organised, self-disciplined and reliable. These skills, in turn, can improve self-esteem, build the resilience to say 'no' to risky behaviour, bridge gaps between the generations and improve the support networks available to young people.

This enthusiasm has faced the expected challenges in terms of evaluation of these outcomes. There are only a very few comparative or longitudinal studies available of the impact of youth services on young people. The range of activities supported by local authorities is vast, from film-making to computer courses or midnight basketball. The range of potential outcomes is also considerable but rarely easily measurable. The programme is currently monitored under a 'Public Service Agreement' (PSA 14) and progress is measured mainly under a National Indicator 'to increase participation in Positive Activities', and other indicators of reducing

- the numbers of young people not in training, education or employment (NEET)
- the use of illegal drugs and alcohol
- under-18 conceptions
- the numbers of young people entering the Criminal Justice System for the first time.

This complex set of outcomes is measured through Tellus2, a national online survey of young people's perceptions administered through a sample of schools (Tellus2 2007). While the means of monitoring the outcomes of constructive activity programmes may well change over time, at present the survey enquires about leisure-time activities and volunteering, together with a range of other questions around education, health and wellbeing such as bullying or the use of cigarettes, alcohol or drugs.

It is clear that this is a very broad-brush approach. It gives some indication of young people's activities and views in a given area but it will not provide information about the contribution of particular activities or individual providers to the overall outcomes. The statutory guidance on Positive Activities indicates that local authorities are expected to involve young people in local evaluations and to introduce their own local measures of progress, particularly for young people in need or at risk, and for certain forms of provision (Department for Children, Schools and Families 2008). Meanwhile, the government is introducing arrangements (particularly through the Centre for Excellence and Outcomes in Children and Young People's Services), to 'coordinate local, regional and national evidence of "what works" to create a single and comprehensive picture of effective practice' in delivering children and young people's services (Centre for Educational Outcomes 2009). Support will be made available both to improve commissioning and develop quality standards for integrated youth support and youth activities, presumably on the basis that high-quality provision is likely to improve outcomes.

For individual young people, the evidence of progress is likely to be seen in small steps in the growth of confidence and self-esteem, as well as the development of practical and social skills. Individual providers bidding for positive activity contracts are likely to be asked for evidence of effectiveness in securing progress and positive outcomes with young people. The commissioning process means that even statutory services, such as schools or Youth Services, cannot assume that they will provide the activities because the voluntary organisations and the private sector (such as sports coaching companies) are now competitors in this 'market'. Even in this diffuse and complex field with multiple potential outcomes, we return full circle to the need for each organisation to be well prepared to evaluate its activities and to develop its own evidence of the ability to produce successful outcomes.

As we see it, the fervour for specifying outcomes and designing services to meet them may, like the value of shares, go down as well as up. The political capital gained from announcing a new drive to improve outcomes in a particular service can be badly dented by evaluation showing that the improvements have not been realised or the costs of the programme are prohibitive. The emphasis on achieving better outcomes is, however, highly unlikely to disappear altogether and the concept of monitoring the results of spend on particular interventions is now well and truly embedded in our systems of administering public services. Despite the practical challenges it presents, it is crucial that we grapple with it.

Activity

Here are some major questions for thought and discussion around the vast array of welfare services working with people.

- How are the shifts towards an emphasis on outcomes, and the commissioning of services to achieve them, evident in your own field of provision?

- Is your organisation affected by the commissioning process?

- Are you currently asked to report on outcomes?

- Is your work affected in any way by the targets set for you?

If you were a government minister with the context of the enormous costs of welfare provision (health, schooling, work with offenders, help for the unemployed, and so on), how would you go about balancing the needs of clients with the requirements for efficiency, value for money and service improvement?

Outcomes and the commissioning process

Your role as a practitioner may not be easy but spare a thought for the commissioners! They have an immensely difficult job. Those involved in some way in the commissioning process will be mostly officials of large organisations such as local or central government, strategic bodies or trusts but they may also be politicians or volunteers representing an interest group or the local community. They have to shape the services that are needed and purchase the wherewithal to run them.

One way to think about this is to imagine you want a winter coat. You might buy on impulse but more usually you would think a bit about the sort of coat you need. You will decide whether you want it for special occasions or everyday use; whether it should be long or short; whether made of wool or synthetics; whether shower proofed or not; in what colour range, and so on. Having 'specified' in your mind what you are looking for, you will go shopping, comparing the coats on offer with what you want and how much you can afford. Then you will buy (or procure) your new coat and hope it gives you pleasure and good wear.

Imagine for a few minutes that you are trying to buy provision for cancer prevention or support services for children with disabilities. The process is essentially the same but is clearly light years away from buying a coat in terms of scale and responsibility. The coat, in the worst-case scenario, can go to the charity shop and your personal budget will be tighter. The service will affect the lives of thousands of people and cannot so easily be changed or 'dumped' and very large amounts of public money may well have been wasted.

Worse still, you have to decide priorities. To continue the analogy, do you most need a new coat or to save up for a summer holiday? And if the service needed is not available, commissioners have to design what is required and provoke the market into providing it (rather like pushing designers of coats to produce sophisticated designs in larger sizes as the number of obese people steadily increases).

Commissioners then have to ensure a fair process for purchasing the service and monitoring the results.

Commissioning is still an emerging art. The Department of Health, in its guidance on what it calls 'world class commissioning', admits that 'put simply, it is a statement of intent, designed to raise ambitions for a new form of commissioning that has not yet been developed or implemented in a comprehensive way across any of the developed healthcare economies'. (Department of Health 2007, p.2)

Commissioning means the entire 'cycle of assessing the needs of people in a local area, designing services and then securing an appropriate service.'

Procurement means those 'specific aspects of the commissioning cycle that focus on the process of buying services, from initial advertising through to appropriate contract arrangements.' (Office of the Third Sector 2006, p.4)

Scanning across various government guidance for commissioning in different fields, however, reveals strong agreement about the essential elements of the process. What the Audit Commission calls 'intelligent commissioning' involves the stages set out below. (Audit Commission 2007; Compact 2009; HM Government 2006; NHS Information Centre 2008)

Analysis and planning

- Being clear about the outcomes to be delivered
- Analysing and understanding local service needs, looking at national indicators for comparison
- Consulting local people about their needs
- Identifying any gaps
- Designing or re-designing the services required to meet them
- Considering priorities and resources to fund the services needed
- Planning how to secure the outcomes and prevent crisis needs in future.

Sourcing

- Commissioning user-focused and *outcomes-based services*
- Understanding the market and what providers can supply
- Developing the market where necessary
- Designing an appropriate procurement process
- Improving processes (where that is required)
- Ensuring that the most appropriate service provider is chosen
- Checking on the quality and quantity and value for money of what is provided.

Monitoring and review

- Assessing performance against the original objectives and benchmarks

- Identifying any changes needed for future commissioning and any adjustment to outcomes

- Getting feedback from service users

- Monitoring and reviewing the performance in relation to outcomes.

It should, by now, be evident that commissioning is a huge and complex process. It offers the possibility of improving the quality of life for local people in very significant ways. The phrase 'place-shaping' has been coined to describe the extensive powers and influence of local government and its partners to set an agenda for improvement and bring about change in a local area through the commissioning of services (Cozens *et al*. 2007, p.6 and p.23). The potential is enormous; the responsibility for both commissioners and those that provide services is immense.

Positioning your agency for commissioning

You can do a great deal to put your organisation in a good position to cope with commissioning processes and funding applications. Think through what you do best and identify your selling points. Do not be tempted to apply for contracts just because they are advertised; be clear about the essential mission of your agency and stick to it. As a provider, you can also play an active part in the partnership structures that surround the process of determining the desired outcomes and designing commissioning processes: being pro-active can help to keep you informed and give your agency a reputation for being cooperative and committed. If you do decide to apply for contracts, the brief guidance that follows may help.

- Obtain a full copy of the requirements of the tender, commissioning process or funding scheme and the application form. Sometimes you will need to send in an Expression of Interest (EOI) or complete a Pre-Qualification Questionnaire (PQQ). These early processes simply establish that your organisation is reputable and sufficiently well managed to be capable of doing the work. Keep the items that may be needed for PQQs on file. You will be asked for items such as

  ○ audited accounts

- ○ your constitution or a description of your organisation's place in a local authority structure
- ○ the company registration number
- ○ details of any charitable status and charity number (if applicable)
- ○ a list of the members of the Board or Management Committee
- ○ copies of insurance certificates
- ○ health and safety, risk assessment and equal opportunities policies.

If your organisation does not have these things in place, it will be a priority to build your infrastructure before you can enter the ring to compete for contracts.

- Read the requirements with great care. Don't skip anything that is asked for: most bids fail because they do not supply the necessary information. Make sure that you are clear about the outputs and outcomes you can achieve. There is plenty of guidance available to voluntary organisations and small businesses on fundraising, service level agreements, contracts and tenders (for example, Business Link 2007; Turton 2006; Whiter et al. 2006).

- Prepare for the commissioning climate by collecting evidence of need for your particular service and keeping an eye on relevant research.

- You need good budgeting systems that are realistic and include all the resources needed to deliver the service adequately. Voluntary organisations should build in overheads such as management time or administration: the principle of 'full cost recovery' has been agreed in principle at least by government (HM Treasury 2002).

Most importantly in this context, you can prepare for commissioning by building evaluation into everything you do. You need regular monitoring processes to produce project data such as attendances or hours of service delivered. You need evidence of successful outcomes in the past, if possible with the client group in question. You also need to be able to state clearly how you propose to produce that evidence for the service for which you are bidding: you require an evaluation plan.

Gathering evidence of outcomes serves two purposes in relation to commissioning: it provides a 'track record' of past work that goes beyond superficial client satisfaction or selected case studies and also provides answers to the questions about whether the project has been effective in contributing to the overall outcomes. We cannot emphasise enough the advice that evaluation should not be an after-thought. Deal with it now and embed it in the systems of your agency if you want to be well placed in the current climate.

Randomised control studies – their value and their challenges

Even when you have a well-developed evaluation system, you can still encounter problems. Even if outcomes are clearly achieved and easily measurable (such as clients entering jobs or obtaining new qualifications) it is rarely possible to be certain that the change was brought about by your organisation alone. There are almost always other partners contributing, or influences at work from family or peers. It may be that your client found a job because a brother pestered a friend to offer him an interview in his business and not because your programme developing job-readiness 'worked'. In prevention programmes, it is particularly difficult to say definitively whether something 'works' or not. It is not always possible to observe what people actually do (for instance, whether they are still smoking or whether they always wear a seat-belt in a car). We can record what they say they do or intend to do but 'proof' of changed behaviour is another matter. Time and resources usually place practical constraints on what you can do in terms of evaluation and even if you produce statistically valid findings and evidence of positive impact at a significant level, it is still not 'proof' in any sense that the programme works – it is just valid evidence that the intervention is very likely to be making a positive contribution.

All that does not stop people asking for evidence that a programme will be effective, that what you do is working, that it is worthwhile. In these days of tight budgets, commissioners do not want to invest in multi-million pound contracts that will not produce the outcomes they are looking for.

Governmental organisations increasingly look for the 'gold standard' of evaluation, which is usually taken to be the randomised control trial. Sherman and others, who compared the impact of various interventions with offenders, have argued that this sort of research design produces the highest level of evidence of effectiveness possible (Sherman *et al.* 1998). In this sort of study, each participant (individual or school or group, etc.) is randomly assigned to an experimental or a control group. The random assignment removes the differences between the groups because the external factors are randomly distributed between the two groups. So if there is a statistically significant difference, you can say that it is down to the programme under examination. We are well used to this method in clinical trials of drugs, where half the group of volunteers are randomly selected to receive the drug and half just get a placebo. With a sufficiently large sample, you can be reasonably certain that if the drug makes people better in the trial, then it will also do the same for the rest of us in the general population.

The problem with this approach is that such studies are immensely costly: in some fields such as health, they will be funded by large commercial concerns like pharmaceutical companies but in other service areas the business interest will not be as highly developed. Some control studies are funded by government agencies but this has been more frequent in the United States than in Britain. Some areas of enquiry are simply not amenable to the randomised study because various considerations prevent the selection of a truly random group where only half the participants will receive the intervention. The Department of Transport, for example, admits in its own guidance on evaluation that road safety education will not normally be amenable to randomised control study (Department for Transport 2004).

In road safety education, as in most other forms of prevention, it is therefore not that easy to say with certainty that a programme works or does not work. It is not possible to sit in every car and observe what the driver does or to watch every child cross the road. People may tell you that they have changed their views on safe driving but you have no means of telling what they actually do all the time. There are many other partners like the police and road engineers who are part of the effort too and it is hard to separate exactly which intervention caused any particular effect. Crucially, in the road safety context, it is almost impossible to envisage a situation where a randomised control study could operate. Most schools or even participants select themselves in or can opt out. Parents might have ethical objections to a move to place their child in a control group that would be denied safety advice. A second option may be to adopt a quasi-experimental design to compare a group who received an intervention with another that did not.

Such difficulties have not prevented commissioners looking for 'evidence-based practice' with the highest levels of evaluation, evidence behind it and in some cases (such as methods for parenting education and support) approaches with such evidence have been imported, usually from the United States, where money has been available for large-scale control studies, and implemented by commissioning bodies in place of locally developed programmes.

Practice example

Staffordshire Fire and Rescue Service contributes to road safety education in the county along with other partners including the police, the Youth Service and Victim Support. Fire and Rescue Services play an essential part in road safety as they rescue injured people, cutting them out or lifting them from crashed vehicles. They also have a general duty to promote community safety in their areas. In Staffordshire, the team use a hard-hitting road safety presentation entitled 'Crash Course', which is delivered mainly in schools to 15 and 16 year olds, before they learn to drive but when they are already frequently travelling with novice drivers. Young people are a prime target for road safety education as such high numbers of this age group are killed or seriously injured on the roads. Over a ten-year period to 2006 in Staffordshire, 40 per cent of all road collisions involved young drivers aged between 16 and 25, while this age group accounted for only 10 per cent of the county's driving licence holders.

The partners commissioned an evaluation in order to find out more about the effectiveness of the programme and its impact on the young audiences. Appropriate design presented a real conundrum for the evaluators as although the county figures on the numbers killed or injured in the area were falling, it was not possible to attribute the change to the educational programme in isolation from other partnership efforts. Moreover, given the practical difficulties of potentially denying the course to selected young people, the time constraints, the absence of any accessible complete list of young people from which a random sample could be drawn, and the problems of obtaining an adequate response from a postal questionnaire, a full randomised control trial was out of the question.

Both qualitative and quantitative methods were therefore adopted. All schools receiving the Crash Course in one term were invited to administer questionnaires to pupils with questions on knowledge, attitudes and self-reported behaviour both before and after they had seen the presentation. All the schools that booked the course for the following term were similarly asked to survey pupils who had not yet received the course. The second cohort of schools effectively provided the 'control group'. This meant that comparisons could be made on a large sample of pupils between those that had received the intervention and those who had not. Comparisons were also drawn between the knowledge, attitudes and reported behaviour of those who did receive the course both before the presentation and approximately one month afterwards. All the pupils were in a similar age band and they came from a wide variety of schools across the county. Characteristics of age, gender and the estimated level of deprivation in the school catchment area were all coded so that these elements could be matched to determine their influence. Statistically significant differences were found showing some improvements in the group that had received the course in terms of knowledge of road safety issues, and attitudes towards safety measures such as wearing seat-belts. There were also identifiable shifts in awareness and attitudes from before the course to after it. The methods and the size of the sample enabled the evaluators to conclude that there was a very high likelihood, not attributable to chance, that the Crash Course was contributing to a greater level of knowledge and more positive attitudes towards road safety in the young people who received it (see Chapter 7, Samples, Practice example).

These findings were reinforced by qualitative interviews with teachers and other stakeholders and in focus groups with the young people. It was clear that the young people could articulate what they had learned and that most now intended to change some aspect of how they behaved in cars on the road. Some could detail ways in which they had actually changed their day-to-day behaviour.

(Hoggarth *et al.* 2009a unpublished)

All that said, you must not go weak at the knees. The range of methods used in a funded evaluation may seem daunting but your organisation does need to have the means to assess the difference its programme is making. Even if it is at a lower level than the major research studies, it needs to demonstrate that it makes a contribution to achieving the intended outcomes. It becomes more not less important to invest in evaluation. It can make the difference to whether a useful programme is able to continue at all, let alone whether it can be improved or developed.

The chapters that follow aim to help you understand the terminology that is used in commissioning for outcomes, and will offer you a sequence for planning your evaluation and practical methods you can use. As a result of reading these you should be better equipped to bid for funding, enter into discussion with commissioning bodies and make a reasonable job of preparing a practical plan for evaluation in your organisation.

CHAPTER 3

Identifying Outcomes

In the first two chapters we explained the current emphasis on outcomes and offered several examples of the stress on 'what works' and on providing evidence for the results of our interventions. In this chapter we get down to the detail of understanding what outcomes actually are, how to recognise and define them and their importance in the present planning systems for social provision. This should help you to handle the terminology and clarify the outcomes that you wish to evidence from your work.

Outcome models

The commissioning process starts and ends with outcomes – the benefits and changes intended from the programmes in which investment will be made. It is a deliberate cycle of planning to invest resources with the aim of improving the life chances of service users.

If you run a profit-making business, your aim is usually simple: to make money for yourself or your shareholders. 'Growing the business' is seen as desirable as long as expansion brings sufficient eventual profit. It means spreading to new markets, opening new outlets, taking on more staff. For some companies, like the great supermarket giants, there seems to be no limit to the appetite for growth.

Public services, in contrast, exist (at any rate in theory) to serve. They are provided to help people in some way that makes a difference to the quality of their lives, whether directly or indirectly. In the past fifty years or so, public services have been expanding at a dramatic rate as the State took on more and more responsibility for the welfare of its citizens. In that situation, many service managers lost sight of the simple essence of their purpose. The sign of a 'good' manager became the ability to expand his or her empire, taking on more functions and gaining staff. Pay became related in many cases to the responsibility for budgets and numbers of staff. The social study of organisations, or simple observation of how people behave, offers a wry view of how much we value the symbols of rank and status in the institutionalised responses like the larger desk, the carpet, or the private office. In some cases, these growing empires lost focus and the quality of service did not keep pace with their size.

Outcome models have blown a brisk, refreshing wind across ineffectiveness and empire-building. What matters is the difference you make, the results you achieve. It is insufficient to argue that you work hard, or that you care a lot, or that people enjoy coming, or even that you are extremely important – the point is whether or not positive outcomes result. The size or length of history of an organisation is virtually irrelevant to the main question of whether or not it brings about the benefits it is designed to produce.

Outcome models go under many different names – for example results-based accountability, logic models, outcomes frameworks, logical frameworks or log frames. If you search on the Internet under terms such as 'outcome models' or 'outcome planning' or 'logic models', you will see the variety of systems and supporting material (and some of the main models are listed in our references – see, for example, Friedman 2005; Penna and Phillips 2005; United Way of America 1996). There are differences of emphasis but they all make the same point: that what matters is the ability to identify the changes you want to achieve, to invest resources to achieve those outcomes and then to evaluate whether or not they have been achieved, before starting the cycle again. They all turn the conventional management approach upside down. Instead of starting with the resources available and deciding how to deploy them (as often as not on more of the same) the process must start with outcomes. The models are often termed 'logical' because they use the simple logic of investing in those services and interventions that you believe will achieve the necessary changes identified from a rational analysis of needs.

To offer a practical example of how this process affects our planning, we can look at the provision of holiday play-schemes for children. In the usual approach, a manager might suggest that if the organisation had another two play leaders, provision could be offered in the Easter holidays as well as in the summer. The application for funding might well argue that play provision would reduce vandalism and anti-social behaviour in the neighbourhood because the children would be constructively occupied.

Outcome planning models: methods for developing outcome-orientated, integrated services

There is a difference between this:

Outcomes ⇒ Activities ⇒ Outputs ⇒ Input of resources

And what most agencies normally do:

Input of resources ⇒ Activities ⇒ Outputs ⇒ (and possibly) Outcomes

---

If you take an outcomes approach, this is the wrong way round because the first question should be 'What is the outcome you want to achieve?' If the desired change is a reduction in anti-social behaviour, the next question is 'What intervention or group of interventions would best achieve this and is there any relevant evidence that might help to answer that query?' Assumptions that our own service or methods are the most appropriate for the situation should be parked on one side until a proper debate has taken place about what approach would be most likely to achieve the outcome. The most effective route to reducing minor crime might be to invest in more park wardens, change the routes of the beat police, offer family trips away from the area, or open the swimming pools at a subsidised price for children. Offering more play-schemes is only one possible solution. The neighbourhood partners need to decide together what provision to put in and, importantly, they then need to evaluate the effect of the scheme they choose on the problem they are trying to solve.

The same principle applies to interventions with individuals. The first step is to clarify the change we are hoping will occur and, ideally where possible, to arrive at a shared view of that with the individual. If a pupil is behaving aggressively in school and disrupting class teaching, the desired change may be to modify the behaviour to a point where the pupil can remain with his peers and learn successfully. The potential activities or interventions in this case are numerous and the choice of action will depend on the analysis of need, available resources and the cooperation of the pupil. The intervention chosen should not be simply the measure that is most often used in such circumstances. Possible interventions might include mentoring, additional activities outside school, an anger-management course, more teaching support, assessment of potential behavioural or learning difficulties, or medication. The intended outcome and the analysis of need should lead the question of what activities are to be provided, not the other way round. The manner in which the outcome planning models change our perspective has been described to us by one practitioner as the process of 'learning to stand on your head': it is a profound change for many of us.

The significance of outcome models for service providers

In Chapter 2, we described the process of commissioning and how those responsible for this will be identifying local needs, and prioritising the changes and improvements they want to see for local people. They will debate the evidence on which interventions are most likely to produce the intended effects and then they will seek providers who can supply those services effectively.

As a service provider or project manager, your piece of the jigsaw needs to lock into this picture. To be best placed to do that, you need to know the answers to the following questions:

- What are the desired and intended outcomes in your field of provision? What changes do local and central government want to realise in this area? What outcomes do charitable funders wish to see?

- Are these outcomes part of, or informed by, major policy initiatives?

- Where is the evidence of need on which these outcomes have been based?

- How do your organisation and your work fit in with these outcomes? Can you show how your provision helps to achieve the desired changes?

- Which body plans services and makes the choice of outcomes in your field? Where can you find the plans and follow their developments in order to be informed about needs and targets that might affect your own agency?

If you are *not* briefed on these questions and watching the development of local plans, then your organisation will not be systematically in a position to apply for funding and take on contracts. You will be forced back into *ad hoc* responses that will only intensify the impression you have of being at the whim of a capricious system. Gaining some sense of direction and control for your agency in the commissioning context will involve you in understanding the local processes of setting priorities and, above all, the outcomes that need to be achieved.

What are 'outcomes'? Understanding the vocabulary

Outcome and logic models have a language of their own: in fact, the various models often use terms in slightly different ways. You need to arrive at a basic grasp of the main terms and take time to think through how they apply to your particular practice situation. You will then be able to handle discussions about service planning or grant applications with much greater confidence. In turn, you will be able to structure the evaluation of your results much more effectively.

Outcomes are the answer to the 'So what?' question: 'So what difference does it all make?' They are the changes or benefits for individuals, families, organisations or communities. They may be short term, medium or long term. Examples would include changes in knowledge, in practical skills, in behaviour or capacity. For example:

- A child may stop 'kicking off' in school and may then avoid being excluded.

- A child may learn to read or to share things with other children.

- A young person may stop carrying a knife.

- A homeless person may be allocated a flat and manage to live independently and sustain the tenancy (which is invariably the result of earlier outcomes such as learning to manage money or reducing drinking).

- A whole community might start an allotment and grow their own fruit and vegetables, thereby improving the appearance of the area and the diet of local families.

All these scenarios are examples of outcomes. We have to ask 'What's the difference? Who is better off here?' We have to learn to look for such outcomes not just the *quantity* of outputs. It is outcomes that have now become the centre of the planning process.

Outcomes can, of course, be negative too.

- You might be working very hard and delivering to hundreds of schools but your prevention programme might be so boring that people are completed turned off and refuse to treat the issue seriously.

- A surgeon might complete dozens of hip replacements and meet all the targets for waiting times and numbers of operations but the patients will not see that as valid achievement if they are left in pain and still unable to walk easily.

Don't assume that effort necessarily means a positive outcome.

In order to produce outcomes, agencies and individual projects inject 'resources': they allocate staffing or money or facilities. Those resources enable the agency to provide some form of activity or intervention aimed at realising the intended outcomes. These services and 'activities' will obviously vary enormously from one agency to another depending on its methods and mission and the results it is aiming for. The amount of service delivered constitutes the 'outputs' of the programme – such things as the number of clients contacted, the number of clinical procedures undertaken, or the numbers attending the scheme, and so on. Resources, the activities in the programme and the outputs are all 'servants' of the aim of achieving the outcomes.

Outcome models are now in common use. You therefore need to be able to follow discussions using these terms and to use them correctly in documentation about your own agency. It is also important for any partnership that is planning services to work at a mutual understanding of the terms and agree how they will be used. We offer some definitions below that are drawn from some of the main work on outcome planning and evaluation.

OUTCOMES

The Kellogg Foundation defines outcomes as 'the specific changes in program participants' behaviour, knowledge, skills, status and level of functioning' (W.K. Kellogg Foundation 2004, p.2). This definition can apply equally well to all age groups and types of service. Mark Friedman talks about 'results' as being identical to outcomes or goals at community level. 'A result is a population condition of wellbeing for children, adults, families and communities, stated in plain language. Results are conditions that voters and taxpayers can understand. They are about the wellbeing of people in a community, city, county, state or nation.' (Friedman 2005, p.19)

The United Way model defines 'outcomes' as 'the benefits for participants of programme activities'. This rather glosses over the fact that 'outcomes' can, as mentioned earlier, be negative too and so what may be more helpful is the broader definition of them as 'the changes, benefits, learning or other effects that happen as a result of your work…wanted or unwanted, expected or unexpected.' (Cupitt and Ellis 2007, p.6)

The terms 'outcomes' and 'impact' are also sometimes used interchangeably to denote the effects that programmes have. We feel that it is generally more helpful to think of 'impact' as being 'longer term' but what really matters is that people working together should agree on how they will use the terms.

IMPACT

Impact is the 'effect of a project at a higher or broader level, in the longer term, after a range of outcomes has been achieved.' (Cupitt and Ellis 2007, p.6)

ACTIVITIES

Activities are what we do to achieve that change, such as providing youth activities, producing health-information leaflets or offering educational programmes to offenders. Projects can be offering very different activities depending on their aims, their intended audience and their specialist area of work.

OUTPUTS

Outputs are the tangible products of the project, such as the numbers of students or the numbers of information packs distributed. They are counted to describe and quantify the size of the programme. That applies both to activities (for example, how many sex education sessions were offered) and to participants (who was reached, how many people came to the sessions).

INPUTS

Inputs (called 'investments' in some models) are the resources that go in to make the programme work, such as money, time, workers, vehicles or facilities.

INDICATORS

Indicators are those things you can read or see or hear that relate to whether or not you are achieving the right results or making progress towards your outcomes. You can use the indicators you feel are appropriate to gather evidence for the achievement of your outcomes. For example, you might choose to use the local crime rate as an indicator of whether the community is becoming safer or not. (The use of indicators is a very important part of evaluation and will be much more extensively discussed in Chapter 6.) Clearly, you need to know how much you have achieved and the direction in which your indicators are headed. Here the term 'baseline' is often used to describe the point from which we have come or what the particular measure was when our activities first started. The concept can also be used to point out where we are headed if action is not taken. Friedman and others often use the term 'turning the curve' to mean success in changing the outcomes *away* from the negative direction in which they are headed into a curve or graph in the positive direction. Results – in other words –are not always a linear point to point improvement but a gradual shift in the direction of the graph. (Friedman 2005, pp. 56–59)

This may seem a rather sterile set of definitions. It is not too difficult, however, to become familiar with them, especially if you work through examples of the terms applied to your own work. The essential point of all this, however, is not to become an expert in technical definitions but to get used to making distinctions between:

- the resources you put in
- the activities and outputs you deliver, and
- the effect of all that effort on your participants.

As we keep reminding you, the central questions for evaluation are 'What difference does it make?' and 'Is anyone better off?'

	Inputs	Activities	Outputs
OUTCOMES →	→	→	→
The benefits or changes for participants that occur as a result of the activities, such as: • greater knowledge • new skills • different behaviour • changes in attitudes • changes in population conditions.	Resources allocated to the programme, such as: • staff salaries • staff time • volunteer time • money • premises • equipment • vehicles • in-kind support.	What the programme offers to fulfil its mission and achieve its outcomes, such as: • provide counselling • offer sports coaching • teach computer skills • offer heart-disease prevention advice • mentoring of offenders.	The quantity of the products of the activities, such as: • numbers of clients counselled • numbers of coaching sessions • student numbers on computer courses • numbers of patients attending coronary prevention • numbers of offenders receiving mentoring.

FIGURE 3.1: AN OUTCOME MODEL

Identifying and defining the outcomes for your project

As a first step, we now recommend that you make sure you can apply these terms to your own work. In Figure 3.1 we show how outcomes occur in a programme as a consequence of the inputs, activities and outputs, with examples of what those factors might cover. It is adapted mainly from work on outcomes by United Way of America (United Way 1996.) Do bear in mind that the best planning starts from identifying the outcomes. The activities you choose and the amount of resources you put in should be determined by the results you want to achieve.

Activity

Using Figure 3.1, consider your own day-to-day work and plot its intended outcomes, its inputs, activities and outputs. Many workers have never thought seriously about what changes they are seeking to bring about or why they use particular activities. This will help you get to grips with the definitions and will also begin a useful discussion about how your project works.

Draw up a form in four columns. Under 'Outcomes', list the benefits to your project users or clients: the changes you are seeking to bring about. In the next column, under 'Inputs', list all the resources that go into the work, remembering to show the in-kind contributions such as volunteer time. Show the focus of the work, the activities or interventions you offer under 'Activities', and, finally, list the 'Outputs' you aim to achieve with some target numbers.

Keep this listing for reference later when we come to the question of evaluating whether or not your chosen outcomes have been achieved.

A well-defined outcome (Dartington-i 2006, p.2.) is usually a statement that covers:

- what is being addressed (e.g. the aspect of the client's progress or the particular conditions in a local area)
- who will benefit (e.g. an individual, or a group in particular need, or a whole community)
- the direction of change (will the measure increase or reduce?)
- by how much it is predicted to change, and over what time period.

If those elements are clearly stated at the beginning, it is much easier at the end to judge what has been achieved.

It is not easy to think through what you intend to achieve and express it as a precise outcome statement. Few projects achieve total precision in their stated outcomes but it is well worth trying hard at least to remove the worst of the vague and unachievable. Some people find the SMART acronym helpful – there are variations in what this is used to stand for but it is usually used to point to the need for Specific, Measurable, Achievable, Realistic, and Time-related targets or outcomes. In Table 3.1, we offer an example of working all this through.

TABLE 3.1: AN EXAMPLE OF A PROJECT 'OUTCOME'

A hypothetical project aims to improve children's health and wellbeing. It does this through a whole-school approach to healthy eating, exercise, the dangers of smoking, and so on. Set out below is an example of designing a precise outcome around the issue of diet in order to answer the key questions of definition. A project like this will, of course, have several other outcomes to work on but, ideally, each one should be clearly defined.	
What is being addressed?	The need for children to eat the Government-recommended intake of five portions of fruit or vegetables per person per day to reduce the risk of some cancers, heart disease and other chronic conditions.
Who will benefit?	Boys and girls aged 8–11 at six schools in one Parliamentary constituency.
Will the measure increase or reduce? (The direction of change.)	The proportion of children with a sufficient intake of fruit and vegetables will increase.
By how much is it predicted to change?	The proportion will increase by 30 per cent from the baseline established with a survey of the children in April 2009.
Over what time period?	By March 2011.
Outcome: By March 2011 an increase of 30 per cent will be achieved against the baseline position at April 2009 in the proportion of children aged 8–11 at the six schools in the scheme eating the recommended five portions of fruit and vegetables per day.	

Many agencies and projects are so immersed in the business of delivering services that they do not step back to consider the outcomes they intend to produce. Some organisations will have a long history of provision in a particular field, and it is not uncommon to come across charities founded in Victorian times with over a hundred years of service. The services of these organisations may be excellent but sometimes the basic reason for their existence has misted up with the passage of time and staff cannot articulate 'why' they do the work or what they are trying to achieve. New people come into an organisation; new projects are added to the portfolio: the purpose can begin to drift or the collective understanding of the aims may falter. The statement of aims can become fossilised: we do not stop to value what we achieve in our day-to-day work. We may have such a well-rehearsed statement about what we do in our profession that we stop thinking about the underlying rationale for our work. However, far from being a chore, it can be exciting to stop and analyse our aims and the difference we make in our work. As one youth worker put it:

> We talk about it all the time. I've just helped so and so and he apologised for swearing. So and so picked up a work book, all that sort of thing which in combination marks tremendous progress...
> We are very bad at recording because it is so everyday to us. We don't value that in ourselves: it's so ingrained in our ethos and our philosophy we take it for granted...we overlook it because that's what we're here for. (Merton, Comfort, and Payne 2005, p.29)

The advent of commissioning and service-level agreements has brought mission, purpose and outcomes back into sharp focus. Although this is driven by outcome planning often the impetus derives not from theoretical or philosophical reasons but from the practical inability to reach firm contracts or agreements if outcomes are not clear. Time spent in an organisation revisiting purpose and outcomes to ensure that they are current, clear and understood by those involved at every level in the work is time well spent.

Practice example

The Wildside Activity Centre is a small charitable project based on the canal side in an urban area in the West Midlands. It mainly provides adventurous activities, such as mountain biking or climbing, and environmental education for children and young people. A narrow-boat gives access to the waterways and the nearby countryside. The project's chief source of income for about twenty years has been a grant from the local authority, which has been supplemented by smaller fixed-term projects and fundraising.

The Board of Trustees is intent on keeping up to date with trends and closely in touch with the local authority requirements. The moves to commissioning and outcome evaluation were anticipated and discussed in detail. In 2007/8, the Centre piloted new evaluation forms with a view to collecting better evidence of its outcomes. The forms were simple enough for the youngest child but allowed the older ones to develop their responses. They concentrated on satisfaction with the programme, evidence of new learning and of intended changes in behaviour with four questions.

- Did you enjoy it?

- Would you do it again?

- Did you learn anything?

- Will what you learned change what you do from now on?

The Annual Report for 2008 was able to set out some of the results, stating that the findings provided evidence of contributing to the outcomes of *Every Child Matters* and to the aims of the local authority.

> In particular, the children's comments on the Summer Programme indicate that (depending on the child and the activity), they have taken part in physical exercise, re-connected with the natural environment, been stimulated to awe and wonder, seen how to take a greater responsibility for the environment, developed a greater understanding of risk and how to control it and learned new things in new ways.

When the letter arrived from the local authority stating that all grants were to be reviewed and that a move to the commissioning approach would replace grant-aid over a transition period, the staff and trustees were not surprised. Service level agreements (SLAs) were to be issued which reflected the outcomes to be achieved and their relationship to the Council's priorities. The form to be completed for the review asked for the activities of the project, the outcomes, how those outcomes related to the priority targets for the city in the Local Area Agreement, and how the Centre would evidence that the outcomes had been met.

The Trustees and the Project Manager debated their response over several meetings, with work between meetings to refine each part of the response. The SLA form went through six drafts before submission. The Board revisited its mission statement to ensure that it encapsulated the Centre's purpose and rationale. The proposed outcomes were arranged under the five outcome headings of *Every Child Matters*. Considerable time was spent identifying as precisely as possible the local targets and national indicators (NIs) to which the work of the Centre related. The Project Manager set out a timetable for the evaluation of different elements of the programme in order to try to ensure that the stated outcome measures would be produced on schedule.

This work was not an academic exercise. The Board members and project staff knew full well that the Centre's main income could be reduced or withdrawn if the proposed SLA was not satisfactory. Every word seemed to count, from the statement of the Centre's mission to each activity listed and every outcome chosen. In a small project providing a wide range of activities that are voluntarily chosen by participants an equally wide range of potential outcomes applies. The Board had to ensure that what was stated in the SLA conformed to the vision of the Centre and did not simply cite local targets in a scatter-gun attempt to secure funding. Past experience and best estimates of future outputs were used to decide the targets. Moreover, each outcome and the measure stated had to be achievable: fix the targets too low and it might appear as if the organisation does not deliver sufficient value for money – fix them too high and the promised evidence of outcomes might not be forthcoming. Good intentions would be insufficient as even with an agreed SLA, neglect of evaluation during the year could mean that the outcomes could not be evidenced. The situation is constantly developing and shifting, demanding vigilant management attention.

Extracts from the SLA that was submitted are set out in Table 3.2 to show how selected outcomes were defined and how they would be evaluated over the part-year remaining, together with two examples from the section showing how these related to the local priorities. For brevity, the full range of outcomes and indicators is not shown here.

TABLE 3.2: EXTRACT FROM WILDSIDE SUMMARY OF ACTIVITIES AND OUTCOMES

What will be the outcomes of your project?		
Across the project, the outcomes will be measured against the five aims of the *Every Child Matters* Agenda. These aims can also be applied to the adult visitors.		
National Aims	Activities	In the year 2008/09 (July to March) the Centre will demonstrate the following outcomes:
Be Healthy	Promoting physical exercise and a healthy lifestyle	60 per cent of participants completing evaluation forms on the adventurous activities will have undertaken at least two hours of exercise at the Centre, and will report enjoyment of the physical exercise involved and a wish to continue with some element of the activity.
	Building individuals' self-confidence and self-esteem	50 per cent of participants on the problem-solving and teambuilding exercises will report an increase in self-confidence and self-esteem. In addition, a proportion of users from the Centre's full range of activities will also be able to report qualitative evidence of increased confidence.

Enjoy and Achieve	Creating the opportunity to learn new things and have new experiences	60 per cent of participants in the educational activities and the holiday programmes will report having learned some new information or skill and/or having had a new experience as a result of their visit.
	Promoting an awareness of the natural environment	50 per cent of young people participating in school activities and holiday programmes will have learned something new about the natural environment.
	Having fun whilst achieving new goals	60 per cent of participants will report enjoyment of the activity they participated in. 20 per cent will also report achieving a new personal goal for themselves.
Make a Positive Contribution	Provision of opportunities for volunteering	At least 700 hours of volunteering opportunity will be provided and supported.
	Providing opportunities to develop teamwork, leadership and co-operation skills	Qualitative evidence will be gathered from the volunteers, the Duke of Edinburgh's Award participants, and young adult participants on the team-building activities. 25 per cent will report an increase in teamwork, leadership and cooperation skills.
	Encouraging visitors to take responsibility for themselves and the environment especially by promoting the 'Reduce, Recycle, Reuse' initiative and working towards Eco-Centre status.	50 per cent of participants in the educational activities will report an increase in awareness of their responsibilities towards the waste they produce.

*Percentages given above all refer to the percentage of those who complete evaluation forms

How do your outcomes contribute to targets for the City? (These targets begin with the Community Plan but are found in more detail in plans for the delivery of services within your area of work including the Local Area Agreement.)

The outcomes we generate as a Centre through our activities contribute to targets for the City both directly and indirectly in many ways. We have identified below those specific targets in the City's plans where we make a direct contribution.

TABLE 3.2 (CONTINUED)

By promoting healthy and adventurous activities, opportunities for cycling and other exercise, and by providing activities which are both fun and relaxing to reduce stress, we contribute to:

Community Plan theme	*A Healthy City*
Local Area Agreement	H2: Improved health for children and young people.
LAA/ Community Plan indicators	H.2. 4 Percentage of 5–16 year olds who spend a minimum of 2 hours per week during term on high-quality PE and school sport within and beyond the national curriculum. H.2. 5 Percentage of young people participating in sport that continue to participate regularly in sport after intervention is complete.
Targeted Priorities 2008	NI 057: Children & young people's participation in high-quality PE & sport.

By working towards Eco-Centre status, and promoting enjoyment of the natural environment, recyling and the benefits of alternative transport, we contribute to:

Community Plan theme	*A Green City*
Local Area Agreement	G3: Improved sustainability in consumption, production and management of waste.
LAA/ Community Plan indicators	G.3.4 Number of kilograms of household waste collected per head. G.3.5 Ecological footprint of the City.
Targeted Priorities 2008	NI 192: Percentage of household waste sent for reuse, recycling and composting.

Choosing outcomes and specifying targets for SLAs and grant applications makes for real dilemmas for every voluntary organisation working with people at the current time. While on this occasion the Wildside Activity Centre proved that attention to detail paid off in continued support, the local authority targets have already changed and funding processes have been adapted to current constraints. Improvements and adaptations will be made in the Centre's plans. The Board cannot sit back and regard this painstaking process as a finished task. They must 'watch this space', constantly monitoring developments in the Local Authority's priorities, targets and spending plans.

Outcomes at different levels – seeing how you contribute to the whole

It is very important not only to identify the outcomes you expect to produce from your work but also to locate them in the overall efforts to produce positive change. Mark Friedman makes the point that outcomes may be large-scale changes for whole communities or benefits on a smaller scale in the lives of individuals. He calls the process of working with partners to achieve such major changes 'population accountability' (Friedman 2005, pp.24–26). The partners will be planning together and making joint efforts to improve outcomes (results) for people in communities, cities, counties, states and nations. The process involves the partners in:

- identifying the population in question

- assessing needs

- defining the results they would like to see (such as a clean environment or children succeeding in education)

- choosing indicators to give a measure of any change

- monitoring the results.

The outcomes are changes in the conditions and circumstances of whole communities.

The other half of the results-based accountability framework is about the separate performance of each agency, project or service. It asks how effective the organisation is in delivering the outcomes it is set up to achieve. These may be with individuals, families or communities. The question of 'performance accountability' can apply to any organisation, from health services, education, environmental improvement through to sport, the arts or business. Friedman suggests four critical dimensions for assessing the performance of an agency (Friedman 2005, p.67):

- The quantity of effort: How much was provided?

- The quality of effort: How well was the service provided?

- The quantity of the effect: How many customers or clients are better off?

- The quality of the effect: What percentage or proportion of clients are better off and how are they better off?

We shall return to these questions in the discussions on creating an adequate evaluation but for the time being it is sufficient to note that these questions concern outputs and levels of satisfaction with the service but most importantly, the quantity and quality of *outcomes*.

Both logic models and results-based accountability are helpful in showing us that outcomes achieved with individuals and groups contribute to the whole picture. If everybody is working to the same overall outcomes, the efforts of individual projects, schools or hospitals, local authorities, regional bodies and national government departments will all fit together. Small changes achieved at one level all add up. The changes at different levels fit together like a set of Russian dolls, contributing to the change that is needed for the whole area. This is sometimes termed 'vertical integration'. Properly used, such models can describe the contributions of different partners in bringing about change in complex programmes.

Few individual organisations or projects will be able to claim that they can show that their work caused a change at *population* level – and it can come as a tremendous relief to project workers to realise that this expectation is unrealistic. It is possible to show evidence for changes in individuals and groups that are contributing to the whole pattern but with most complex social problems, no agency is going to be able singlehandedly to make the difference to the population-wide factors. We have encountered workers who work with individuals and small groups sinking into depression because they feel that evaluation of their work can never show achievement on the major targets featured in strategy documents. If you work with children to help them learn to read, you will not be able to show that you changed the literacy levels in the population as a whole. You should, however, be able to show outcomes in improved reading ability and confidence in the group with whom you work, and can realistically argue that this difference will contribute to the major goal. A treatment agency working with Class A illegal drug users should be able to show the numbers of their clients who have stopped using and how long they have been 'clean'. It cannot show that it has achieved the national target of reducing use of the Class A drugs but every user whose habit has ceased contributes to the overall picture. The evaluation task becomes much more manageable when a project or service breaks down what it does under the headings of 'intended outcomes', 'activities', 'inputs' and 'outputs'. Instead of focusing on ultimate impact or population conditions, it is possible to define the contribution that the project can realistically make with its own users.

Practice example

In 2005, the Scarman Trust (now Novas Scarman) was commissioned under the Single Regeneration Budget to provide a scheme aimed at reducing gang involvement and gun crime in a neighbourhood of Birmingham where crime mapping and community consultation had shown up major concerns. While gun crime in Britain is still low on international comparisons, violent crime does have a devastating effect on local people and Birmingham ranked amongst the cities suffering most from shootings resulting in deaths and injuries. The aim of the Project was 'to contact young people at risk of involvement in gang-related activity and the use of firearms and to involve them in programmes which challenged their behaviour and offered alternatives to their lifestyle, with the ultimate goal of reducing their offending and enhancing their educational achievement and employability.'

The Project was designed to identify 80 young people aged between 11 and 25 who had been identified, through outreach or referral, as at risk of gang activity and to involve them in a programme of activities such as mentoring, youth activities, sports, groupwork and educational programmes in basic skills and personal and social education. Those assessed as most at risk received the most intensive interventions. The Project worked closely with other agencies to respond to the identified needs of the young people, making links to education and training, employment opportunities, drug treatment, conflict resolution and other appropriate interventions

The scheme had a clear rationale based on the evidence that educational underachievement and family and peer pressures are major contributors to young people's offending and that, conversely, educational qualifications and employment are particularly effective in providing routes out of criminal behaviour. For those involved in gangs and gun crime (most of whom are from particularly deprived neighbourhoods) getting a job often seems totally unattainable and self-esteem and social skills are poor. Many had not been attending school for months or even years. To achieve even small steps of progress, intensive personal and family support and educational and recreational activities to build confidence and skills would be needed. As most of the clients were likely to have a complex set of needs an holistic approach would be necessary, involving a referral system and a range of different partner agencies.

It was clearly unrealistic to claim that a small neighbourhood programme could affect the numbers of firearms crimes recorded in the city. Causal relationships would be hard to demonstrate even within the neighbourhood. It was, however, possible to take a lead from the rationale for the project and demonstrate real steps into learning and employment for those with a high level of assessed risk. This realistic approach meant that output and outcome measures could be designed that were proportionate and reasonable to expect the Project to attain.

The original application for funding set out the measures to be adopted. Output targets included numbers of participants engaged, the number of hours of activity for each client and the number of participants who sustained involvement with the Project for at least six months.

The main outcome targets were:

- to achieve involvement in full-time schooling, training or alternative education for 80 per cent of clients aged up to 16

- to achieve a 33 per cent reduction in the numbers of those aged over 16 who were not in education, employment or training (NEET) compared with the situation at their initial engagement with the Project

- to achieve a 50 per cent reduction in arrest rate for the core group compared with the 12 months prior to their engagement with the Project.

The setting of these outcome targets enabled the Project to set up a data base from the start to record such things as numbers of clients, their assessed levels of risk, their hours of involvement and activities pursued, educational qualifications gained and entry into training or jobs. In the event, data on arrest rates proved difficult to access but qualitative evidence of changes in risk behaviour and gang involvement were available from interviews with clients. The Project was thus able to show that, amongst other achievements, 37.5 per cent of the clients over 16 had obtained employment or entered training in some form by the end of their involvement with the programme. The project's initial work on setting realistic outcome targets paid off in the clarity of the final evaluation.

Table 3.3 offers a schematic continuum that may help you clarify the relationships between immediate and longer term outcomes and how they build up over time, and between change for individuals and cumulative change for communities. You should note that the categories are not cut and dried in real life and blur into each other to some degree. For example, although learning often does happen in the short term in some cases it takes longer and occurs in the medium or even long term. Equally, although some changes in behaviour may happen immediately, generally speaking behaviour is the hardest thing to change. The list of potential outcomes listed is, in any case, not exhaustive.

TABLE 3.3: OUTCOMES – A CONTINUUM

Short term	Medium term	Long term
What are the short term results or outcomes?	What are the medium term results or outcomes?	What are the long term results or impact?
For individuals	For individuals	For individuals:
• New learning • Increased awareness • New skills • More knowledge	Changes in: • Attitudes • Feelings • Opinions • Motivation • Aspirations • Behaviour • Actions • Policies • Decisions	Changes in: • Life chances • Employment prospects • Personal health • Improvements to income and economic position • Personal safety
For communities and populations	For communities and populations	For communities and populations
Increased awareness of what constitutes, for instance, healthy or safe behaviour	• Changes in behaviour in families and groups • Greater social acceptance of positive patterns of behaviour	• Changes in individuals, families and groups lead to population results such as: • Improved social conditions • Economic health of the area • A cleaner environment • Improvement in rates of disease and mortality • Greater safety and less crime

Understanding what individuals gain from a programme

Many of us have become used to evaluating our interventions in terms of how well an activity went and tend to think of evaluation as solely concerned with this aspect of the smooth running of the work, the users' enjoyment and their satisfaction with it. Now that we are required to concentrate on the outcomes of changed awareness, skills or behaviour, we need to evaluate our programmes not only in terms of the activities they offer but also in relation to what participants gain from them. Clearly, the outcomes for individuals will vary and will be at different levels and occurring at different stages for each person. However, it can prove useful to ask people what they achieved in terms of what they know, what they can do or do better, and how they may think or feel differently about themselves and others. They may well also be able to tell us how they apply what they have gained elsewhere in their lives. Stakeholders such as parents, employers, teachers, local residents or the police may also have relevant things to tell us about how our work with our users has influenced their own work or the wider community.

In Table 3.4, we present a model of evaluation based on the thinking of Kirkpatrick and other writers. (Hamblin 1974; Kirkpatrick 1959; Merton, Comfort and Payne 2005) This is concerned with a results-orientated approach to evaluating training programmes. We use it here to identify the focus of enquiry into the effects of an activity or intervention at four levels. We have also set this against the notion of a time-frame for the type of reaction that might reasonably be expected immediately after an

TABLE 3.4: EVALUATING THE EFFECTS OF AN
INTERVENTION – A FOUR-LEVEL FRAMEWORK

Level	Title	Focus	Does this show outcomes?	Time-frame
Level 1	Reaction effects	Satisfaction and recommendation/s for change	No – not routinely although may include request to identify some gains	Immediate
Level 2	Learning and development effects	Gain, change, achievement, progress	Yes – generally knowledge, attitude change, insight and understanding. May include other gains as well	Short term
Level 3	Behavioural effects	How learning/gains are applied elsewhere	Yes – likely to be behaviour, actions taken, things put into practice	Medium term
Level 4	Effects on others	How the gains have affected others	Yes – other people's views can show up the direct and indirect benefits to stakeholders, the family or community.	Long term

intervention, shortly after it or in the medium or longer term. The notions of short, medium and long term are, of course, relative and it is useful to identify for your own project what these might mean in actual periods of time. Some funding requirements can mean that long term is, in reality, within quite a short time period.

Level 1 (*reaction effects*) focuses on participants' satisfaction; what they liked about the programme and what they think should be changed. We are generally familiar with this sort of evaluation; it tends to be what we are asked about in a number of situations – from going to the theatre to completing an online training module. It focuses on assessing our responses to what we have experienced and asking us for any suggested improvements. Gathering evidence of satisfaction rarely generates good evidence of outcomes; people can enjoy a programme without achieving any real change for themselves. Outcomes tend to be evidenced at levels two, three and four of this model.

Level 2 (*learning effects*) focuses on what participants identify as the benefits and gains for themselves. As noted above, in the short term at the end of a programme, this is likely to centre on what participants know or understand and maybe how they feel and think differently. Such outcomes can include what are often termed 'soft' outcomes (as explored in Chapter 6) and might include growth in confidence, motivation and aspiration.

When learning is put into effect through action or changed behaviour and participants apply what they have learned in one setting elsewhere in their lives, this is evidence of level 3 (*behavioural effects*). With a crime-prevention programme, for instance, young people might learn more about how dangerous it is to carry a knife and how little this will actually protect them from injury or situations where they can be in trouble. They might work on a role-play about resisting peer pressure. One member of the group might then apply his learning outside school on his own housing estate by refusing to carry weapons like the rest of his 'gang'. Outcomes such as having developed greater assertiveness and ability to resist group pressure might also be considered as soft outcomes. These might be viewed as ends in themselves or as steps on the way to contributing to a wider policy goal such as the reduction of knife crime.

Finally, what in this table is entitled level 4 (*effects on others*) is the evidence of how what we do has an effect beyond the participants who are the direct consumers of our programmes; it is evidence of what others may see as benefits to them or their work. In this sense it shows up the multiplier effect of how our provision benefits other services or individuals. The families of those with whom we work, or stakeholders within the local community, often have views of what we do and are often very willing to

Activity

In relation to your own work, identify which of the levels shown in Table 3.4 you think your own current evaluations cover.

If you discover that your current evaluation only covers level 1 satisfaction and reaction measures rather than outcomes at other levels, spend some time identifying how you might gather evidence of outcomes at levels 2, 3 and 4. Think how you might find out:

- what people know or understand, or how they see themselves differently, as a result of the activities you offer (level 2)

- how they behave differently or do things differently (level 3)

- the indirect benefits of your work: that is, what other people say about the effect of your work on their situation (level 4).

tell us if they have experienced benefits or can see the difference in the behaviour of others.

This exploration of the different types of outcomes and the levels and time-scales on which they are reached does not provide watertight categories. What it should do, however, is help you to think realistically about what your own work can be expected to achieve. There is no point claiming that outcomes will be achieved that are not in fact feasible in your particular situation or on the given time-scale. This will simply result in failure and embarrassment and an inability to construct clear evaluation measures. It is better to locate what you do realistically and show how this contributes to the wider achievement of outcomes at population- or community-level. You will probably find that going through this process releases you to find better ways of gathering evidence for the outcomes you *do* achieve.

CHAPTER 4

So How Do I Start and What Do I Need to Think About?

Making a plan – answering the essential questions

The message we want you to hear from this chapter is that the best evaluations are well planned long before the project even *starts*. We have established that commissioners are likely to want to see evidence of the outcomes of your work. Not infrequently they also make it clear that they will not fund evaluations by external researchers and that you must ensure that you have ways of assessing your outcomes within your day-to-day work. In 'real life' however, you are quite likely to arrive in a job or take up a project leadership position without a clear idea of how the work is to be evaluated. You may even have been in a role for a long time without having any clarity about the sources of funding or what is required in terms of evaluation evidence. The first step is to find out what has already been written down on the subject and whether there is any current evaluation and, if so, who is responsible for carrying it out. If there is a vacuum in relation to these questions, you need to start some planning yourself and to begin to influence others to take evaluation seriously.

At this point some people lose confidence that they can cope with what they see as being a complicated academic process. However, if you are capable of working with people in the complex interactions that establish trust and produce real change in their lives, then it is well within your grasp to collect some evidence of those outcomes and plan a means of reporting

Activity

How much do you know about the evaluation process in your own organisation? Are you confident that you know what outcomes are intended from the work and how those are evaluated? We suggest that you try answering the following questions to test whether or not there is an adequate evaluation plan in place.

- Where are the intended outcomes of your project or agency documented?

- What are the funders' requirements for evaluation evidence?

- Who is responsible for planning and delivering that information?

- Have there been any evaluation reports in the past and are these available to look at now?

- Is there a budget for evaluation?

- Is there a plan that tells you what data is to be gathered, how and when it will be processed and what your personal responsibility is for contributing to evaluation?

If you draw a blank on most of these questions – it's time to get planning!

it. There are helpful books and resources on the Web that can help you and several are listed in our references, for instance, Ellis 2005; McNamara 1997; Taylor-Powell, Steele and Douglah 1996.

Finding good evidence of outcomes does not happen by accident: it happens as a result of systematic planning and it is a continuous process of refinement. It is therefore critical that you take steps now to develop your own plan. 'So where do I start?', we hear you asking. We now describe the essential steps for your planning process and if you take time to work through these questions, you will stand every chance of producing a sensible, achievable plan. (The same principles apply if you are contracting external evaluators but here we will be assuming that someone in your own organisation is undertaking the work, as that will inevitably be the case with some part of your need to show outcomes.) Each step will then be explained a little further, with pointers to where more detail is found in other chapters.

The critical steps for planning any evaluation are set out below:

- Decide *why* an evaluation is needed.

- Think about who its *audience* will be.

- List the *activities* undertaken in your organisation or area of work.

- List your expected *outputs*.

- Decide what *outcomes* the intervention hopes to achieve, and express them clearly.

- Consider what *indicators* might show those outcomes.

- Think about what *methods* could be used to find evidence on those indicators in-house, or get a full methodology from the external research team.

- Decide *what needs to be done, by whom and when* to find the evidence.

- *Analyse and write up* the evidence you have gathered.

- *Use the report* as appropriate with partners and to make improvements to the initiative.

Why is the evaluation needed?

The most frequent answer to this question will be that those who fund the work or its partners want to know whether the programme, treatment or initiative is working to produce the changes it claims it is producing. That is the question of the overall outcome of the programme. As discussed in Chapter 1, there may also be other reasons for needing an evaluation instead of, or as well as, the need to evidence outcomes. These other questions do need to be thought through before starting work as they may require particular sorts of information to answer them:

- Sometimes there are pressures around resources and a need to determine which programmes produce good value for money.

- There may be queries about the content or methods of the programme, how to improve it or develop it in future or how to replicate it elsewhere.

- Organisational structures can also be an issue, with questions around whether these are appropriate and effective for producing the desired results.

- Sometimes there are questions about the needs of particular target groups, such as young women, offenders or residents in certain neighbourhoods, and what methods are effective in meeting those needs.

The exact focus should be clearly set out before designing or commissioning an evaluation.

Who is the intended audience?

The intended audience for your evaluation is also a key issue, and one that will inform your design. This raises questions of what answers these readers are likely to be looking for from the report and of what material they are likely to read and absorb. In terms of interest in particular issues, commissioners and politicians will usually want to know which initiatives are likely to be effective in producing the changes they have identified as being of top priority. Almost everybody will take an interest in the targets to which they themselves have to work in their own particular service. Prison personnel, for example, would be interested in managing people while they are in custody, programmes that change behaviour and the end-results in terms of reductions in re-offending. Schools may have a particular interest in pupil attainment on their central curriculum.

Some audiences, particularly national bodies with responsibility for large programmes, will have an expectation of robust research and statistically valid findings. Others will find that type of information too 'academic' and will be more interested in qualitative examples that bring the work to life. Think about how much information people are likely to read, and then adjust your plans for writing it up accordingly. It is always a good principle to avoid jargon and technical language but this is particularly important to remember here because most people reading your report will be lay people, probably unfamiliar with the detail of what your work involves. Make sure the report speaks in ordinary language and offers enough background to make it easy to understand what your project does. If your report is necessarily a long one, then consider providing an 'executive summary'. If you are aiming at media coverage, you may need to emphasise those parts of your report that speak to currently newsworthy issues, or rewrite your findings in a more digestible form.

What are the activities provided?

It is necessary to be clear what specific activities are offered in the programme under evaluation as this detail answers the questions people ask about what you actually do to try to achieve your aims. Even where projects share a single purpose, their activities may be very different. For example, in the field of work that aims to reduce domestic violence, activities in one or several projects might include family therapy, educational programmes in schools, provision of refuges, counselling and advice, police protection schemes, television advertisements, and so on. Interventions may be offered to individuals or to large or small groups in different settings. They may be part of a partnership effort or undertaken by a single agency. For the purposes of evaluation it is necessary to be clear about what constitutes the activities of the programme and which elements of the programme are to be covered, if not the whole. It also helps if, at some point, the rationale for including the activities is set out as well as how they should contribute to the intended outcomes. If, for example, drama activities are offered to young offenders, it is worth spelling out how it is argued that these will contribute to reducing offending and whether other research shows evidence of a similar effect.

What are the expected outputs?

A description of the coverage of the programme and its expected outputs is also needed. This should include such information as the age groups served, settings, types of need, and geographical coverage. The output targets will deal with such measures as the number of patients or participants, the number of leaflets distributed or sessions delivered. Don't be tempted to stop collecting output data in the face of the current increased stress on outcomes. Output information is useful in three respects:

- It helps to provide the audience with a clearer picture of the size and scope of the programme.

- Later on in the evaluation process, it will guide the question of sampling, (which is further explored in Chapter 7).

- It will also be needed if 'value for money' questions arise as it is quite conceivable that an intervention could 'work' brilliantly with the participants but be much too expensive to resource for the overall numbers needing it.

What outcomes is the intervention hoping to achieve?

A clear outcome evaluation will be able to state at the beginning what the programme aimed to do – what difference was envisaged as a result. The list of outcomes should be capable of being matched to findings in the evaluation about how far each one was achieved, if at all. It should give the reader a direct answer to their questions about what evidence can be offered that shows whether this intervention works or not. Your evaluation should genuinely enable an outsider to know whether or not the proposed outcomes have been achieved, even if the answer is not always positive.

If you have worked through Chapter 3 on how to identify your outcomes clearly and precisely, then this should not be a difficulty and you will have the list on file. Very often the outcomes will have been stated in the original funding application, although perhaps less clearly than you might now wish. It is very important to include the objectives of the relevant funding in your report but you may need to restate them as measurable outcomes to make the task of producing good evaluation evidence easier. In some cases, the service may simply be working to the relevant national targets and so detailed outcomes will not be already in place. Evaluators will then need to clarify what outcomes are intended before they can look for any measures on which to gather evidence.

If the intended outcomes are clearly stated at the beginning of the work, it is very much easier at the end to judge what has been achieved. It is also much easier to plan the evaluation as indicators will need to be chosen and data gathered for each outcome listed. If you are listing a claimed outcome but have no means of gathering any information about it, then your plan is in some trouble and you need to revisit your ideas about what data to gather.

What indicators could be used to show a contribution to those outcomes?

Unfortunately outcomes do not come with ready packaged measures. We may not be able to measure the progress directly: we may have to choose what indicators we will use to say whether or not the outcome has been achieved. Indicators are usually seen as proxy measures – for something you cannot measure directly, you find an indicator which tells you about it and arguably gives you some measurement. For instance, it is not possible to tell with certainty what a person's attitude to smoking really is but it would be reasonable to take one indicator of attitude change as movement towards disapproval on a scaled question asking how bad smoking was for their health. Similarly, while we can only guess at what people's real intentions are it would be reasonable to take as evidence what people say in a focus group about how they intend to behave, such as whether or not they are likely to try to give up smoking in future. The choice of indicators is a critical part of both planning for outcomes and evaluating achievements and is best done at the beginning of the process rather than when you are already at the evaluation stage. (This is so important that we offer more advice on how to choose your indicators with more practical examples and activities in Chapter 6.)

At this point it is worth asking someone to read through your planning thus far – you could ask another member of staff or a volunteer or board member to do so. The point is that the outcomes listed, the indicators you have chosen and the means by which you intend gathering evidence about them should make sense and be easily understood. If this seems obscure to others at this stage, or if the data to be gathered does not obviously relate to the outcomes, then go back and think again. There is no merit in being over-complex. This is a straightforward process that should seem like common sense to a lay person.

What methods could be used to gather evidence on those indicators?

The range of potential methods is vast and includes:

- quantitative methods, such as surveys, scoring techniques or analysis of available statistics

- qualitative approaches such as interviews, group processes, observations, or free-text comments.

The choice of methods should be informed by practicality and by what would make a credible evaluation for the audience concerned. The many options will be further developed in Chapter 7, where we will take a look at the literature on the pros and cons of the different methods.

Remember that you can gather good evidence by building your evaluation into your programme design so that it is an ongoing process. You do not always require external researchers. Some measures can be used on a regular basis, such as outcome-related questions on the normal evaluation sheet for each session or scores on periodic tests. Some other useful evidence will probably also be available already from case records or client files such as notes on assessments of progress or the response to particular interventions.

To collect evidence of outcomes, there are three basic approaches, as described below:

MEASUREMENT OF AN INDICATOR AGAINST A BASELINE

This is often used to show changes at whole-population or group level and uses quantitative data – for instance, the number of children born with a low birth weight compared with the number in previous periods, or the number of drink–drive convictions year on year.

MEASURES OR DESCRIPTIONS OF CHANGE OVER A PARTICULAR PERIOD OF INTERVENTION – AT THE BEGINNING AND AT THE END, OR BEFORE AND AFTER

These may be quantitative measures taken at two points in time such as an attitude test of young people's views on how acceptable it is to use cannabis or cocaine before and after a drug prevention programme. They may also be qualitative descriptions of the change conveyed – for instance, by a case study of an isolated mother who has received support from a family support worker and who is now much less depressed, has enrolled on a training course and is better able to communicate with her children.

RETROSPECTIVE JUDGEMENTS ABOUT WHAT PEOPLE FEEL HAS IMPROVED

These are opinions gathered about what people feel when they look back. They are judgements about what feels different for them now compared with how they remember feeling before their contact with the project. This might be, for instance, about taking drugs or their confidence to resist peer pressure. Such judgements can be gathered through a structured format or through less formal, qualitative interviews or exercises.

When we collect evidence in these ways it is usually the case that we do not have the time or resources to obtain responses from everybody in the group we are interested in. *Sampling* is the process of selecting a smaller number (of people, organisations or objects) out of the whole group under study. If the sample chosen is a representative cross-section of the group being studied as a whole, then it is possible to make generalisations from the findings about the whole population under study. A more detailed discussion of sampling methods is provided in Chapter 7.

The question of sampling is hugely important when valid statistical evidence is needed. Statistical tests of significance provide an estimate of the probability that any differences observed are not the product of sheer chance – i.e. whether there is a genuine connection between the variables, such as the level of knowledge in a group that have received the programme and a group that have not. For the purposes of statistical significance and validity, the sample must be sufficiently large and representative of the population in question. We will return to the question of sampling in more detail in Chapter 7 and if your evaluation demands statistical validity, the best way forward is to take advice from an experienced statistician at the planning stage before embarking on a study that could fail to show statistically significant findings simply because of poor design.

Try to plan to include a pilot to test your methods and your questions, even if it is only a few participants answering your questionnaires, in order to be sure they are easily understandable before you launch them with the rest of your intended group. The more you can do to test and refine your methods the better. You can also check that the answers can be analysed as you intend. If for instance you need evidence of what people gained from a programme, you might try analysing a few sets of questionnaires to see if the questions, in the way you have written them, and the answers people have given will yield enough material on this topic for your purposes.

What is needed in your work plan?

You need more than an abstract evaluation design: the detailed tasks required have to be addressed to be sure it is achievable, and as a means to checking that it is on track. The work plan needs to address who will do what and when in order to deliver an agreed report in the required time-frame. Internal staff will always have to do some work to support an evaluation even if external researchers are appointed.

The plan also needs to set out any resources or support that will be needed, such as purchase of software or the creation of a database. The rule of thumb is to be as specific as possible about the task, put names beside each job and a date for its completion. Use the plan to check periodically that everything is working well and is on schedule.

Responsibilities should ideally be clearly agreed between staff. Several people may contribute to the tasks of evidence gathering, data input or writing up but it should always be made explicit who has overall responsibility for each element and who has the final decision about matters of content and style for the report.

How can the data be analysed and written up?

We will discuss the approach to analysis and writing up in detail in Chapter 9. However, for now we will simply say that at the planning stage, any particular structure required in a report or questions to be addressed should be set out in advance. The report must then deal with those questions directly and show how the evidence relates to them. The analysis should be based on the signs of progress drawn from the outcomes and indicators chosen. It may be 'quantitative analysis' (for example, the instances of a particular indicator, such as patients saying their pain is reduced or that they sleep better) or it may be 'qualitative analysis' (for example, tracing the comments in focus groups from patients who have had surgery about what helped their recovery). Qualitative material can be analysed for important themes and reported under those headings.

For the purposes of your plan you will need to decide not only who will collect information but also who will undertake computer input if needed, who will analyse the material and who will actually write the report. These are all classic points at which evaluations unravel. Too many organisations can show you boxes full of previous evaluation forms or surveys that have simply never been used. They gathered data without the key planning decisions about whether they had the skills or capacity to analyse it, so the information went out of date and is now of no practical use.

Most grassroots workers feel that they struggle with writing reports, but try not to let this become an obstacle if this is your own situation – remember, it's not unusual to lack good writing skills. Advice on report structures and on content are available in Chapter 9 and in the resources listed in Appendix B. Remember always to use the spell-checker on your computer when writing up your report. It is important to find the support necessary for the writing-up stage so that good evidence does not go to waste. You may be able to contract a consultant to undertake the final write up or to check and edit what you have produced. Make sure you allow enough time in your production schedule to receive comments and then to restructure your report if necessary.

How can the report be used effectively?

You should not assume that once the report has been submitted to your funders, your own copy will simply sit on your shelf. In fact, your plan should address how the report can be used for maximum effect as a good quality evaluation report can be used strategically. Evaluation takes up valuable energy and should therefore not be wasted. Your report should be used wherever possible to tailor and improve the current programme. It can also be used to argue for resources or gain credibility with stakeholders. It can help to gain entry to particular audiences. Qualitative evidence and quotations can be as effective in gaining attention as statistical information – they tell the story and catch the imagination. Case examples, quotes or statistical evidence can be used (with appropriate permissions) in publicity, in information packs or on websites.

Practice example ————————————————————

The Beacon Councils' Positive Youth Engagement Peer Support Programme was funded by the Department for Communities and Local Government and the Cabinet Office. Its aim was to spread good practice in involving young people in decision-making, planning and volunteering in public services. Twenty-three local authorities were involved in total in the national programme and its evaluation was carried out by the Youth Affairs Unit at De Montfort University.

At the very beginning of this complex contract a substantial Work Plan was negotiated with the Beacon Councils. It set out all the main tasks of the evaluation design, from the literature review, through to survey design, interview schedules, data analysis and writing up with the responsibility for each of them, the timetable and the product expected. There was also a space to identify the assumptions made about how the evaluation would be supported locally. Internally, individual responsibilities were allocated amongst the eight members of the evaluation team. An extract from this Work Plan is shown at Table 4.1.

This preparatory work paid off in numerous ways. The project leader was able to monitor progress against it and to make the necessary reports to the Cabinet Office. Where partners or individual researchers had not kept to the timetable or fulfilled their part of the plan, it provided a record of the original agreed commitments against which new negotiations could take place. The final report was delivered and approved on time.

TABLE 4.1: EXTRACT FROM WORK PROGRAMME FOR POSITIVE YOUTH ENGAGEMENT EVALUATION 2007–9

Objective	Tasks	Responsibility	Provisional timetable	Outputs	Assumptions
Exploring perceptions of young people involved and potentially involved.	Individual interviews and/or focus groups in the course of visits to Beacon Councils.	Evaluators	By Dec 08	Qualitative perspectives and comments.	Beacon Councils and partners will obtain any appropriate parental permission.
	A questionnaire to all young people who have been involved in volunteering, mentoring, consultation, etc.	Evaluators with Beacon Councils	Between Oct 07 and Dec 08	Target is to achieve 250 returns.	Dependent on Beacon Councils and partners to distribute questionnaire and on workers to give it to young people, to encourage response and administer returns. Assumes young people will respond. Help may be needed for disability or literacy difficulties.
	Design questionnaire	Evaluators	Sept 07		
	Distribute questionnaire to young people via projects and partners. Follow up. Post back returns. Data input and analysis.	Beacon Councils / Evaluators	July 08 / By mid Dec 08 / To end of Jan 09	Will ensure opportunity for participants in the schemes to give their views.	

Designing it in

As mentioned earlier, it is important that evaluation is part of the bread and butter of your daily work. For individual organisations it should be embedded in all the processes of planning and management. New projects should build in evaluation from the very start. Good monitoring systems, well maintained databases, and evaluation methods that can be used as part of the daily work can all be effective in saving energy in the long term. The time and effort required pay much higher dividends if evaluation is treated as a core part of the work rather than if it is regarded as an added extra, and there are several reasons for this.

In the first place, there is less energy wasted if all members of staff understand the part they play in evaluation and the reasons why it is needed. If workers have to use evaluation forms as part of their regular work or are required to input certain monitoring information, they need to be briefed about the reasons for this work and how it should be done. Checks should be made periodically to ensure that the required action is actually taking place because it will be far too late to discover crucial gaps when the final report is being assembled. Communication between staff is critical as a good many people besides the key evaluators can be involved in setting up the requirements for gathering data or in collecting information themselves. If people perceive this work as a nuisance or do not realise its importance to the organisation, they will be inclined to forget or omit essential evaluation tasks. Your managers, board or trustees may also need to be included in such communication so that they understand why staff time is being spent on these roles.

Practice example ─────────────────────────────

In a small arts project offering dance and drama for young people in order to raise their confidence and motivation to learn, the project manager introduced an evaluation sheet to be completed at the start of the twelve-week programme and again at the end. The majority of the staff worked part-time, coming in to deliver sessions on a particular dance form or aspects of drama skills. They needed to use the evaluation sheets themselves as the project manager was not always present at these sessions.

There was a good return of evaluation forms at the start of the programme. At the end of the twelve weeks, however, most of the young people had left before it was realised that the second phase of forms had not been completed. The part-time staff had not realised the importance of obtaining the evidence of progress at the end of the scheme. All the design work was therefore wasted on this occasion and no 'before' and 'after' measures could be presented. The report had to rely on a small number of qualitative case studies and fell far short of the credible picture of outcomes that had originally been envisaged.

It is well worth allocating time to explain to staff members, and to work through, the significance of outcomes for the survival of the organisation, the current evaluation plan, and the information to be gathered. For workers, the understanding that every inch of progress that they help people to make contributes to overall outcomes not only helps to make the data-collection tasks bearable but can also make a positive difference to their job satisfaction. As we argued in Chapter 3, it can be a major encouragement to staff to see exactly how their work contributes to the outcomes for the agency as a whole.

Practice example

St Paul's Community Trust and Community School dedicated its whole annual staff away day to the question of outcome evaluation. It was their practice, and an excellent one, to include *all* staff in these events so that teachers, administrators, nursery staff, youth workers, technical and support staff all had an opportunity to discuss their work together. The site maintenance staff were also, therefore, present.

Each contributing team worked hard at defining their own outcomes, what the indicators might be and how they might be captured. At the report-back, the group most excited by the work was the caretaking and maintenance team. Perhaps for the first time, they had collectively realised how essential they were to the whole operation. They were able to show how they did monitor efficiency of response on crucial maintenance factors such as heating, lighting and health and safety concerns. They could show how they tried constantly to accomplish this maintenance cost effectively and in an environmentally friendly way. They could now see that none of the educational outcomes could be achieved without warm, welcoming and safe premises.

The maintenance staff had also realised that in broader ways they contributed to the wellbeing and progress of the students. They could provide examples of offering practical training for some of the young people that had stimulated learning and facilitated re-entry into education. They had a vision of expanding apprenticeships. In some cases, maintenance staff had been involved in mentoring local children or supporting them through family difficulties.

All the staff teams produced similar work on their contribution to outcomes. In many cases, a clearer picture emerged of the necessary linkages between the teams. Morale benefited. The breadth of these contributions was written up as part of the organisation's strategic plan.

Careful design of an evaluation programme at the beginning can mean that the necessary tasks can often be undertaken as an integral part of daily work without a great deal of additional effort and often with positive benefit to the clients. Users can benefit from evaluation that is routinely undertaken during their participation because this can help them reflect on their own needs and be encouraged by their achievements. Assessments are often necessary for other purposes but the activity of discussing assessment can be used not only to identify symptoms or needs but also to identify and mark the evidence of progress. The participatory activities that we explore in the discussion of methods at Chapter 7 are particularly suitable for involving participants in evaluation in a way that can be of benefit to them.

Practice example

Staff in a Sure Start Children's Centre in the East Midlands were keen to find streamlined ways to evidence the targets on which they had to report since they didn't want processes that were unduly burdensome. All staff in the multidisciplinary team therefore reviewed their existing recording systems, looking to include key outcome measures in routine assessments. Staff aimed to include questions in the paperwork they used every day to generate the data required for the Centre's quarterly returns on the national measures.

The example shown in Table 4.2 is from the midwifery team. As midwives see pregnant women routinely, they are in a strong position to gather data on smoking reduction and cessation. When a woman is booked in, her smoking status is recorded together with the number of cigarettes she smokes a day and whether or not she would like support in order to stop smoking. These same questions are revisited at 28 weeks, at the birth and at discharge from the midwifery service. Health visitors continue this tracking when they become involved at a later stage.

Being clear about the measures required – in this case reduction in smoking – and embedding the means of gathering this information in routine work processes has a great deal to commend it. Data is captured as part of day-to-day tasks; it is then already within the organisation and ready to be retrieved as required at reporting periods.

TABLE 4. 2: EXTRACT FROM ASSESSMENT AND REVIEW
FORM USED BY MIDWIVES IN A SURE START PROJECT

Smoking status at booking					
1. Non smoker		2. Contented smoker		3. Concerned	
4. Planning to stop		5. Just stopped		6. Contented ex smoker	
SMOKING					
Did you smoke pre-pregnancy?	Yes	No	Comment:		No. smoked:
Are you currently smoking? (*Booking*)	Yes	No	Comment:		No. smoked:
Would you like some help and support to stop smoking?	Yes	No	Comment:		No. smoked:
Are you currently smoking? (*28 weeks*)	Yes	No	Comment.		No. smoked:
Would you like some help and support to stop smoking?	Yes	No	Comment:		No. smoked
Are you currently smoking? (*Birth*)	Yes	No	Comment		No. smoked:
Would you like some help and support to stop smoking?	Yes	No	Comment:		No. smoked:
Are you currently smoking? (*Discharge*)	Yes	No	Comment:		No. smoked:
Would you like some help and support to stop smoking?	Yes	No	Comment:		No. smoked:

Making sure the plan addresses the outcome questions

When your plan is almost ready, look through it again. Check that the steps proposed will in fact give you information about outcomes by the end of the process. Of course, this should be a superfluous reminder but we have all been so used to reports about the quantity of our work, how much we do, how many people we see and so on, that it is alarmingly easy to lapse back into that mode. Information on outputs has its place but it is not enough.

Try to picture the final report being read by strangers who do not know your work. Ask yourself 'Will this tell them what difference all this work makes? Will this give them evidence about whether people are better off as a result? Will it tell them how many people (and what proportion of them) are better off because of this programme?' We will return again and again to these questions about outcomes. If you cannot say with some confidence at the stage of producing your draft evaluation plan that the resulting report will answer these questions, then you still have more work to do on your plan.

Practicalities and logistics

When you are planning, try to think in simple concrete terms about what is needed to bring the plan to fruition, just as you would if you were putting on a play or inviting twenty people for a buffet supper. You need to think ahead about the resources you will need, including costs, the time you have available and the cooperation you may need in order to achieve your ideas.

Resources

Cost is obviously an important issue and may by itself rule out some methods of evaluation. Face-to-face interviewing is a valid method but if the circumstances mean that it would involve expense and time to travel to respondents who are widely scattered around the country, then it might have to be rejected on grounds of practicality. You need to check that what you are proposing can either be accomplished in-house for minimal cost, that there is an allocation for evaluation in your project budget or that you have the time to try to raise a grant.

If you are considering contracting external evaluators, costs can easily run into tens of thousands of pounds. Freelance or academic researchers will be charging around £3–500 a day or more at current prices to earn their income and cover their costs. This may well be justified for a substantial study at a key point in the life of your project but few organisations can afford such sums for evaluations of every aspect of their work.

If you decide to cover the evaluation internally, it is even more important to spell out the costs and resources needed so that you do not meet difficulties later on. Staff time is obviously the main factor but remember to consider items such as photocopying, postage, reply envelopes, telephone, travel, software, equipment like tape recorders, and the cost of printing the final report. Remember, however, that a relatively small amount of money in each year of, say, a three-year project can deliver a reasonably substantial study if there is careful planning and maximum use of internal capacity, perhaps alongside specific external advice and expertise. If at all possible, budget for evaluation from the very start within the original proposal for new work.

Capacity

Funding is not your only concern. Even given an unlimited budget for evaluation (hypothetically, of course!) you would still need to look at your capacity to carry out the design. It is a matter of the numbers of people available to work on the evaluation and whether or not they have the appropriate skills. Will there be enough interviewers available? Does your agency have people capable of analysing survey returns? If not can you locate suitable external help in time?

Each task links logistically to the next one. The capacity must be in place somewhere to cope with the tasks proposed at the time they are needed. An administrator cannot send out a postal survey if it has not yet been designed by the researchers. For the sake of argument, the survey might be needed while the administrator is on holiday or a worker might need training before they can use a particular spreadsheet to input the results. The most competent report writer may be committed to other priorities at the time the report is needed. Your plan must, therefore, be feasible in terms of the personnel available to carry it out.

Timing

In our experience, particular care is needed in order to be realistic about all aspects of timing. Evaluations are often inadequate because the plan was unrealistic for the time available. Make sure you take particular account of the deadline for submission of the report and work backwards from that date. Each step has to dovetail with what follows. To illustrate this point: if surveys in schools are required it will take considerable time to contact the schools, obtain the necessary permission from the head teacher or head of year, and to ensure that teachers understand how to administer the questionnaires. You will need to accomplish all that *before* any surveys can go out. You will also need to establish a period for completion and a deadline for returns before anyone can analyse and write up the results. Parental permission may be required before young people can be interviewed. A period for reply or opting out will be needed before the young people can be selected and the interviews can start. The tasks of data analysis and writing up can be substantial and as much time as possible should be allowed for them. The final steps such as checking with managers, receiving comments, amending and printing also need listing in your countdown to submission. You will need a work plan with all the deadlines on it or some form of chart setting out the difference phases of the work (Denscombe 2002, pp.67–70).

Try to use time effectively. Some research methods such as face-to-face interviewing are intrinsically time consuming. Setting up interviews and travel to meet respondents can absorb whole days of the time you have available. If it is possible to invite respondents to a central meeting place and conduct several interviews one after another, that will enable you to collect the same evidence in a much shorter time. If there is a significant amount of survey data to be entered on spreadsheets for analysis, it may be more cost and time effective to employ a skilled data-input specialist who can work at speed, than to give the task to someone in house who is not used to such tasks.

Access and cooperation

Even if money and time and capacity are not problematic, your planned methods still need to be checked for feasibility in terms of the cooperation they demand from other people. Put yourself in the shoes of others: they may be too busy; they may be competitors of your project; they may dislike your methods or someone in your organisation. Try to adjust your plan to realistic expectations of the support you are likely to receive. Work with the relevant people to reassure them and find some common ground of benefit that could result from the study, such as improvements to practice or better ways of helping a particular client group.

Be aware that the data that you might find most useful may not be available: it may be confidential or it may not exist in a form that can be easily shared. Such things as personal files of clients or offence records may be extremely relevant but even if access is granted, you may find that the evaluator must gather the material on the premises of the organisation that holds it. Data-protection considerations might mean that files may not be removed. In any case, you will usually have to 'sanitise' any records that are used, which means removing any information that relates to the identity of the individual concerned (see Chapter 5).

Practice example ——————————————————————

An evaluation of the effect of a particular road-safety information programme in schools examined the responses of the pupils using a large-scale survey. It is known that school achievement is affected by deprivation. Relevant issues here are that: the brighter pupils might be better able to answer the questions correctly; affluent parents might be more concerned about the safety of their children, inclining them to treat the information more seriously; peer pressures known to be associated with crime and anti-social behaviour in areas of high deprivation might be influencing the responses; road accidents tend to be more frequent in deprived urban areas.

It was therefore seen as necessary to be able to examine the effect of deprivation as a potential influencing factor on responses.

The evaluation team considered using the free school meals allocation to each school as an indicator of the level of deprivation in that school catchment. This is a measure used quite commonly and is reasonably accurate as free school meals entitlement is assessed each year on various criteria of low family income. However, despite agreement that this would be a useful measure, discussions with the County Council concerned soon showed it was not a feasible way forward as this information was collated at county-wide level and was not detailed for individual schools. It was also a busy time for the local authority and no one was available to work on the data to extract that information in the timeframe needed for the evaluation.

A compromise measure was adopted, using an estimated level of deprivation based on the Index of Multiple Deprivation for the ward in which each school was located. While this was less accurate than the free school meals measure, it had the merit of being practical because all the information required was already available in the public domain.

There are some ways of increasing the likelihood that you will obtain the access you need. Time can be well spent explaining the need for your evaluation and the methods it will use to those who keep relevant information or who can open up access for you. For instance, in a study requiring responses from minority ethnic group parents, it may be necessary to spend time with the elders of that community explaining the purpose of the evaluation and reassuring them about its approach. Such people can function as 'gatekeepers' who can open doors for you. Remember that your own reliability and integrity are at a premium here as any suspicion of broken trust will damage not only your own evaluation work but other people's research efforts as well. People are quite rightly suspicious of researchers and their trust should not be abused or taken for granted.

You also need to imagine what your individual respondents will feel about your approach. If someone struggles with reading and writing then a long questionnaire is going to be very forbidding and they may choose to 'lose it' or just refuse to fill it in. If you are a busy mother or a pressured professional, you may feel that an hour to answer interview questions is precious time you may not want to give away. Some studies use incentives such as gift tokens or additional fun activities for respondents. If used with care, these can be helpful, but if they are to be used, the cost needs to be included in the evaluation budget. Many people will respond if they understand that the evaluation may simply improve services for themselves or others. Sometimes they value the offer of a copy of the report or being informed of the findings. Whatever the situation, at the planning stage, it is important to consider what will motivate others to provide information. The most sophisticated evaluation design is completely useless if people will not respond!

The need for 'objectivity'

We have struggled here for the right words. 'Objectivity' in research or evaluation probably does not exist. It is a fact that the presence of the researcher changes the situation. He or she brings a personal history and a whole set of views to the situation: other people responding to the study react to the outside influence. The questions that are asked and the manner in which they are asked will itself influence people's responses. Indeed, in some forms of research, such as ethnography, the personality, values and perceptions of the researcher are regarded as a valid instrument in the process of understanding what is going on and the subjective insights of the researcher are expected and valued. However 'scientific' the design, it can never eradicate these dynamics entirely in order to capture the perfect picture of what is actually happening. (Denscombe 2002, pp.157–173)

What we want to argue here is that while it is important to acknowledge that position, evaluators should aim towards objectivity, open-mindedness and neutrality in everything they do. Evaluation, particularly of outcomes, never starts from an entirely neutral position. Either the workers in a project will be trying to evaluate their own effectiveness or the evaluation will be commissioned from an outside body that is paid to research the evidence and produce the report. In either case, there is a natural wish to find good results and to reflect well on the project – and there may even be explicit pressure to do so in some situations.

This is all the more reason for looking carefully at the need for objectivity. Some people might call this 'being professional'. Evaluation is more than taking a photograph of our best side. However much we might wish to identify successful outcomes, it will do more damage in the long run to our agency if we cannot be as objective as possible. We might be able, for instance, to persuade our child participants to say they had learned a great deal from the project or we might simply ask a leading question but that evidence can easily be blown out of the water by a child's casual remark or a parent's comment. Closer examination of our methods will reflect badly on the organisation. Equally, we may see that a particular question is producing criticism or negative findings and decide to drop that from the schedule but the effect of this could be that the evaluation looks biased and the agency may never deal with what is going wrong.

Objectivity means neutrality and being open to the evidence. It means being free from bias – or at least, acknowledging bias. However, this is an ideal as all of us bring our own personality and values to evaluation and so complete objectivity is rarely possible. Nonetheless, there are steps we can take, to keep a watch on the issues of objectivity and integrity.

We can:

- be aware of our own vested interests and what a positive report could mean for our own careers

- acknowledge who the sponsors of the evaluation are and what this means in the expectations for results or the pressures on us to produce particular findings

- make sure we look out for contrary evidence and alternative explanations. We may be able to build in external checks on our results

- be honest with ourselves and others about our own prejudices and values. Particularly positive or negative views of certain people or methods should be acknowledged and put to one side

- design our evaluation to test the evidence as rigorously as possible

- avoid research methods that use leading questions, manipulate respondents to agree with our hopes and expectations or do not allow the respondent to choose from real alternatives

- make sure the research process, data and analysis are open and available to scrutiny. Strictly speaking, another evaluator should be able to ask the same questions as you have, use the same methods and then find the same results

- make sure that findings are not artificially exaggerated or minimised when we write them up. There is a place for portraying the best of our work in publicity but evaluation is not journalism. It is not an exercise in spin but in neutral assessment.

The need to prevent harm

When thinking about potential evaluation methods, it is easy not only to be unrealistic but also to spin off into approaches that could have a questionable

Activity

Imagine your project has to complete an evaluation for its funding body at the end of three years. As a project worker, you have made use of a standard questionnaire to assess the gains in learning for your participants. This was agreed by your agency when the evaluation was set up at the commencement of the project.

At the end of the first year, your line manager meets with you to consider the first year results. The results on some of the questions do not look positive. According to the responses, most project users have made little progress in those areas. Your manager suggests that those questions should be dropped from the questionnaire for the second year of the evaluation so that the report will contain results that put the project in a better light.

How would you respond? What arguments can you put forward if you want to keep to the original questions? If you think your manager might be right, are there any downsides to his or her suggested way of dealing with the problem?

effect on your respondents. For example, it could be highly desirable in an intellectual sense on a teenage pregnancy project to have more precise information on the sexual behaviour of the target groups of young women after their participation in the sessions. Such information could help develop findings on whether their behaviour has changed after the intervention. It is very likely, however, that questions about this would be far too intrusive: they could upset the young women or drive them away from the project. They could, in fact, be unethical.

'Ethics' means moral principles or codes and the key principle at stake here is that your evaluation should not do any harm to those who are involved in it or jeopardise their safety or development in any way. When you are planning your evaluation, ethics should, therefore, be considered alongside the methods. Some methods could potentially yield rich information; it does not follow that they are ethical.

There are many sensitive issues involved: for instance, most people who have a criminal conviction may be reticent about answering questions about their past and may not want to be honest with a researcher. If they do respond, they will almost certainly want to know what will happen to the information they give. Nobody can offer absolute rules here but some methods of gathering information will be completely unethical and others require careful thought to be sure that the respondents are safeguarded. In Chapter 5, we set out the main ethical principles that should be considered in each situation and explore how to ensure that they are followed in practice.

It's important that you include in your plan details on how you will deal with the ethical issues raised by the methods you propose.

Needing to prevent harm to individuals is one major reason for careful planning. However, in conclusion, we want to suggest that the same concern to safeguard our users and do the very best to support their progress should prompt us to plan evaluation carefully for many other reasons as well. If the project is making a positive difference in the lives of its users, a credible and well-designed evaluation using effective practical methods will be one of the quickest routes to maintaining the impetus of that work. If it is not effective in all respects, a balanced evaluation plan is likely to show up why that is the case and make it possible to address the problems in the interests of the users. Ultimately, whatever our own agenda may be, we should not be providing more of the same, regardless: our clients *deserve* well-planned evaluations of our interventions in their lives.

CHAPTER 5

Thinking About Ethics

In this chapter we will be unpacking the basic ethical principles that we touched upon at the end of Chapter 4. These principles should inform *all* our evaluation plans and methods.

Safeguarding our participants – the principles

The fundamental principle that informs all other principles is that no one should be harmed by research or evaluation. That may seem obvious – after all why should we want to harm our clients? A moment's thought, however, will remind you of the repellent experiments that have been conducted in wartime in the name of research, or even some of the errors of present-day medical research that have resulted in illness or injury for the participants or have failed to obtain the proper consent of the families involved. This should be enough to convince you that the issues around ethical issues are not always self-evident.

> Whether research is done on people or whether it is done with them there is the possibility that their lives could be affected in some way through the fact of having participated. There is a duty on researchers, therefore to work in a way that minimises the prospect of their research having an adverse effect on those who are involved. (Denscombe 2002, p.179)

Ethics are not an exact science. What is legitimate can vary with the precise purpose of the evaluation and the context but this is not a completely abstract matter. It is a matter of common sense to consider how research might affect the person on the receiving end. You just need to imagine yourself in the shoes of someone faced with a researcher or interviewer: think about what you would want to know and what doubts and worries you might have. The ethics of evaluation are just about putting safeguards in place so that people can respond with confidence and without fear of pressure or misrepresentation. We need to work in a manner that respects the rights and dignity of our participants and to act with honesty and integrity.

Activity

Imagine that you receive a letter informing you that you have been selected to take part in a 'lifestyle survey' conducted by a research company. You think you may have heard the name of the company somewhere or read it in the papers. The letter explains that the research will be very useful in 'identifying social trends' and 'informing government agencies about the need for services in the future'. It says that an interviewer will call at your house on a certain date and encourages you to ask them any questions you may have. The request is for half an hour of your time to answer their questions.

Would you simply welcome this interviewer into your home and answer their questions? Or would you ask questions before deciding, or even refuse to take part?

Jot down what thinking informs your decision and what questions, if any, you would want to ask.

The various professional associations for researchers all publish codes of ethics. The best known for the British context are those for sociologists and psychologists, both of which can be easily accessed on the websites of their associations (British Sociological Association 2002; British Psychological Society 2006). Such codes set out both general and specific principles to inform ethical design and make as certain as possible that those who receive our services or those who participate in our evaluation will not be adversely affected by it. In Chapter 4, we discussed the search for 'objectivity' in evaluation and the issues of pressures on the evaluator and conflicts of interest. Such matters of honesty, integrity and respect are enshrined in the principles of all codes of ethical practice. These overarching principles include the need for evaluators to:

- report findings accurately
- observe legal requirements
- consider their own safety and the safety of their participants

- avoid intimate personal relationships with those involved in a study
- make clear any possible conflicts of interest.

Evaluators should act without discriminating against any individual or groups of people and the matter of inclusiveness is developed more fully later in this chapter. Similarly, the protection of children and vulnerable adults who are involved in any way in evaluation is absolutely paramount and of such importance that it is also separately explored below.

The general principles contain several useful cautionary pointers. We need to be aware of the dynamics of power in the situation: generally speaking, the evaluator will be more influential or appear to have more power than the client of a service – not least because evaluation tends to influence the distribution of resources. If an evaluator argues that a programme is effective, for example, it will often count for more than the views of clients when decisions are taken about future funding. It is therefore necessary to be conscious of how easy it is to put people under pressure, threaten their security or affect their feelings in some other way. We need to be sure that what we are undertaking ourselves, or asking others to undertake, lies within our established competence and skills: if we are unsure, advice or training should be sought. This would apply particularly to experiential exercises or experimental designs that test responses or explore feelings. Our methods should not place unreasonable burdens on the practitioners involved, especially not if this prevents them offering an essential service. In our view also, the use of covert methods where participants are not aware of being studied or of what is actually going on in the study are seldom justified in evaluation of people-orientated services: they contradict the principles of honesty and consent and should be used with extreme caution, backed by expert advice and only where absolutely necessary. The possibilities of a loss of trust or alienation from the service are usually too great to be justified and there are many other methods that can used instead.

Many people will have concerns about whether cooperation with a request to participate in evaluation could possibly bring them any harm or be in some way inadvisable. Most texts on research methods or evaluation list four specific practical principles that should be considered whenever you are setting up evaluation or research. These are the factors that will generally cause people most concern and on which they may want reassurance. Even where participants trust you completely, these principles should be followed to ensure that as far as humanly possible no inadvertent harm or detriment will affect them because they took part. Where there are exceptions made to these principles, you should be sure that they can be fully justified. It might for instance be legitimate to cause some degree of stress to test the result of a treatment if that were the only means of testing available.

The four main ethical issues for all research are developed below:

- *Informed consent*: people need to know what they are agreeing to

- *Voluntary participation*: people need a free choice about whether to participate and to be able to stop or refuse to answer questions

- *Anonymity*: readers of any evaluation report should not be able to recognise the person who gave their views

- *Confidentiality*: others should not know what the respondent said or did.

Informed consent and how to get it

It is sometimes tempting to involve people in evaluation without fully explaining what you are doing. It may seem quite reasonable to tell users, for example, that this is 'just a chat' about how useful they have found the project without ever saying that you are actually engaged in evaluation. Questionnaires or tests are sometimes used without telling the participants about their real purpose, sometimes because time is short or because it is felt that they would thus find the process less intimidating. Such approaches are, however, almost always wrong and unethical. The principle we should be following is to explain what we are doing in sufficient detail and in ways people can understand. They then have a right to *choose* to participate or not based on a clear understanding of the purpose of the evaluation and how it will be used.

People have a right to understand what is going on, who is funding the study, what is involved in terms of methods, who will be collecting their views, what use will be made of them and how their views will be written up. Many people, especially service users, will be anxious about how they were selected to take part. Respondents will want to know what sort of questions they might be asked, how long it will take and whether they can stop if they do not like the process. They need to have control of the decisions about what to say, and to whom, and to be confident that giving their views honestly will not have adverse consequences. If they are to be observed or involved in active tests or exercises they need to have an understanding of what will be involved. Evaluators should make clear whether participants will be able to change their answers or not, add further comments or withdraw their statements. Most participants welcome some feedback on the findings of an evaluation and not infrequently they complain that other researchers never 'got back to them'. They should therefore be informed about whether they will see a draft, receive a summary or have access to the final report.

The process of obtaining informed consent will usually involve writing to participants or offering a verbal or written explanation of the nature of the evaluation before embarking on an interview or exercise. For face-to-face interviews or tests, participants will usually be asked to sign a consent form, though sometimes in group situations a verbal explanation will be seen as sufficient. In any case, it is good practice to offer an information sheet that underlines and backs up your verbal explanation. This can also provide respondents with a contact for queries or complaints – and if they are likely in any way to be disturbed by the questions or the activity, it can offer details of sources of support or counselling. You should always allow enough time for people to ask you any questions that occur to them, so that you can clarify and offer reassurance. The information will cover their rights to refuse participation and to anonymity and confidentiality, with any limits that apply. If the evaluation takes place over a protracted period, consent may need to be sought on more than one occasion as people tend to forget what is involved and exactly what they have agreed to.

With written surveys, the action of the respondent in filling in their answers is normally taken to indicate their consent to the process but a questionnaire should always carry sufficient introduction to provide a picture of the sponsoring agency, the purpose of the study and the ways in which the answers will be used. With telephone interviews, it is good practice where possible to write to potential respondents in advance to advise them of a call, the nature of the evaluation and of their right to decline a conversation. If this is not possible, the interviewer should offer the verbal explanation and make sure the person selected is genuinely willing to take part before proceeding with questions. Even where respondents are happy to respond, a more appropriate time for the call may need to be agreed.

Clearly, particular care is needed when evaluation involves children, young people or vulnerable adults. Issues of age, disability and physical and mental health should all be taken into account. Consent will normally be sought from parents to involve children under the age of sixteen (or from the carers or guardians of adults who may not be fully capable of deciding for themselves or who may be at risk in some other way). This should not, however, be used as a pretext for dispensing with a proper explanation of the evaluation in terms the person themselves can understand: even small children can, and should, consent and should be completely free to refuse or stop if they wish.

It is often the case that parents will not be present when children are interviewed or tested and cannot easily be contacted face to face to explain the study to them. It is usually seen as acceptable to send out letters explaining the evaluation – for example, from schools or service agencies – to all the parents concerned asking them to complete a form or make contact to 'opt out' or withdraw their child. Such a letter would make clear that if they do not opt out, then their child will be involved in the study. It should stress that all the normal principles of confidentiality, child protection and so on will apply. Parents would often rightly expect that those dealing with their children will have had criminal conviction checks and this should be stated in any letters sent out. Examples of a consent form and an information sheet are provided in Appendix A at the end of this book.

Voluntary participation

Nobody should be coerced into contributing to evaluation nor should they be put under pressure to answer any questions they find intrusive, sensitive or difficult. They should also be able to stop or opt out for any reason without any questions or repercussions. They should be confident that if they criticise the project, it will not affect the service they receive. The form of questioning should not be oppressive or insensitive – many people, for example, will be worried about written questions or long words on account of their own problems with language or literacy. Others will worry about giving 'incorrect' answers.

Most of us would assent to this principle of voluntary participation without any difficulty. In most people-orientated services, it would be relatively rare to force any client to take part in anything or to undergo a test or treatment against their wishes. The circumstances where coercion is permissible are usually very tightly prescribed. The problem does not lie with our acceptance of the principle but with the many ways in which we can *inadvertently* put pressures on our clients that make it hard for them to refuse to take part. We can legitimately stress that the evaluation may help the project in the long run but there is a fine line between doing that and suggesting that if users do not assist, the provision may no longer be available. Some workers go even further – manipulating their users by telling them that their response is desperately needed or that negative answers will jeopardise grants to continue the project or affect the workers' future jobs. Many clients will, in any case, be afraid that any criticism could affect how they are seen by the agency and the sort of service they will then receive.

It is also especially important when working with children to remember that as an adult you usually have some authority in the situation. You need to be aware of the pressure a child may feel to conform to your requests just because you are a 'grown up'. If the request is conveyed by someone in a role they would normally be required to obey, like a teacher, then that expectation can be reinforced. It is necessary to spend time carefully explaining that this is a voluntary matter, unlike many of their other activities in school. Depending on the situation, alternatives activities may need to be provided to occupy those who do opt out of an interview.

In the course of an interview or exercise, the evaluator should be sensitive to any signs of discomfort or boredom. It is not enough to explain what is happening at the beginning and then just plough on. The interviewer should stress that the participant can stop at any time, or refuse to answer any question that makes them uncomfortable. A personal question may be phrased with a caveat to emphasise this freedom, such as 'Remember that you don't need to answer this if you don't want to'.

Activity

Mr Parton is now 91. He is in a residential care home operated by a national charity and is generally very happy. His daughter, Emma, is fairly satisfied with the service and glad that her father is happy. She is however becoming concerned about how her father's increasing incontinence is being managed.

The manager of the home has embarked on a survey of relatives to establish their views of the care provided. This will be part of the background information for a forthcoming inspection by the Care Quality Commission, where the manager is hoping to achieve an 'excellent' rating. Emma Parton knows the survey is important. She is worried that if she gives her honest opinion and seems to criticise the care then the staff may be irritated and become less patient with her father.

How could the manager explain the survey to relatives in order to reassure them and obtain honest answers?

Confidentiality and anonymity

Confidentiality and anonymity are related:

- 'Confidentiality' means that information given to evaluators should not be disclosed to anybody outside the evaluation team in a way that can be traced back to the individual concerned. 'Leaks' can be embarrassing or may even put people at risk. People should be reassured that what they say will not be reported in a way that is attributable to them, unless they have specifically been asked about, and consented to, being quoted. Comments from individuals will not be reported: they will be used to report on trends and the overall picture.

- 'Anonymity' means that individuals are not named in a study or report, nor can they be identified by their role or title or any other personal characteristic. If proper steps are not taken to protect anonymity, then matters that were intended to be confidential can be made public as readers may be able to guess who said certain things, and thus confidentiality will be destroyed.

Whether you are writing or talking about your evaluation results, it should not normally be possible to identify individuals. It is crucial that the views, circumstances and life histories that people offer should not be traceable to them as individuals. While this seems on the surface to be sheer common sense it is easy to overlook some common pitfalls:

- Questionnaires should usually make clear that you do not need to know the name of the respondent and so you should consider carefully whether you really do need people's names on your questionnaires before leaving a space on your form for this. Lists with names can easily be left around and it is also possible to disclose identity by mistake.

- Postcodes are extremely useful for the analysis of geographical information but remember that a postcode will identify just a few houses. It may look perfectly harmless to write that 'There is a high incidence of Class A drug use in these postcode areas' but that leads back to a very small number of families who will be easily identifiable.

- Even without a name, other details may also identify an individual – especially if they are unusual in some way. For instance an example given in a report of 'an asylum-seeking family with two children who have made regular use of the project' looks anonymous enough but it could be unlikely that there are many asylum seekers using the agency and so local people will know perfectly well who is being described – it is only human nature to try to work it out.

There are some exceptions to the anonymity principle where for example, you want to attribute quotations or highlight good practice. Where it is possible to identify people in a report by their name or any other detail such as their job title, you must ensure that they have given their permission.

In terms of preserving anonymity, the rules of thumb are as follows:

- Code data against numbers not names. Each respondent should have an individual reference number.

- Do not use the real names of participants in any report, unless they have specifically given permission (preferably in writing). If a pseudonym is insufficient to disguise identity, you may also need to change other key details such as age or gender.

- Do not use photographs of people, even in group pictures, without their permission.

- Do not put specific details in the report in a way that could potentially identify clients or respondents (e.g. addresses, street names, postcodes).

- Avoid any other personal attributes that could accidentally identify someone (such as family details, agency or job role, school, physical characteristics, or neighbourhood details like names of local pubs or 'gangs'). Remember that it is often a combination of characteristics that enables others to identify the individual (for example, that a boy in Year 10 had red hair and was bullied).

Most workers in services dealing with people would say they are fully aware of the principle of confidentiality. The issue is covered in most professional training courses. In that context, it is therefore surprising how often we slip up. You can probably quite easily think of someone who has been hurt or damaged because a worker they trusted betrayed their confidence or because something they wanted kept private was shared outside that relationship without permission. This can happen all too easily in the process of evaluation, albeit often from over-enthusiasm rather than deliberate intent.

If people agree to respond to evaluation questions, they have a right to know that no one else in the organisation outside the evaluation team will know what they said. They need to be sure that if they trust you enough to disclose some of their personal history that it is not going to become common knowledge. It is one thing to reply honestly about your feelings or your background in an interview: it is quite another to take on board the possibility that what you say might become public and colour how others react to you. In most circumstances, we have a right to privacy as individuals – and most of us guard that very carefully.

There is of course an area of exception and that is where issues of child abuse or major crime are disclosed in the course of evaluation and this will be discussed further below. With these exceptions, the general principles for keeping confidentiality include the following:

- Avoid gossip: it can be all too tempting to share the interesting information you have been told.

- Keep notes and information securely (in locked filing cabinets or password-protected files).

- Use a reference number for each respondent, and keep names and details separate from your interview notes or tapes. This means that it will be impossible, or certainly less easy, for someone who comes across such notes to deduce the name of the person to whom they apply.

- Have a written confidentiality policy that can be given to project users and/or explain in the introduction to your evaluation how confidentiality will apply.

- Give the interviewee a choice as to whether they disclose any of their personal details. To avoid this affecting the interview, you may find it helpful to ask for personal details at the end rather than the beginning.

- Give the interviewee the chance to review and change the information given so that nothing is kept on record that they are unhappy about.

- Ensure that a failure to make examples fully anonymous does not jeopardise the confidentiality you intend.

- Be clear with others that you cannot provide information on what people said, even if they feel it would be useful to the organisation or the client concerned.

- Ensure everyone involved with the evaluation understands and adheres to the confidentiality procedures.

Activity

Best practice is to make sure that respondents to interviews for evaluation purposes receive an explanation of the process and sign a consent form. It is a good idea to test this out and rehearse your explanation first in order to ensure it is simple and easily understood in your project context. We suggest that you now try drawing up your own information sheet. Think of a piece of work you might need to evaluate and tailor the document to your practice situation. Make sure it includes information that covers the principles we have spelled out, such as taking part voluntarily, and the rights to opt out and have responses treated anonymously and confidentially. Be clear and give specific details: when participants give their consent to taking part, it should be as a result of having had a thorough explanation that they can understand and, preferably, keep for reference. Remember to ensure that your information states the limits to any guarantees you make.

To help you get started, we have provided some key questions that a participant might ask. These might serve as headings: you may be able to think of others you would want to include.

- What is the purpose of this evaluation?
- What does it cover?
- Who needs the information?
- Who is paying for the study?
- Why have I been picked to take part?
- Do I have to agree to take part?
- If I do, what will be involved?
- How much time will I have to give?
- Could it do me any harm?
- Will people know what I have said?
- Will people know that I took part?
- What will happen to the results?
- We've had a lot of researchers here who don't tell us anything – will we know what comes out of it?
- Who is organising this evaluation?
- What happens if I want to complain or if I have concerns?
- OK, so what happens next?

When you have a draft, try it out. Ask a friend or colleague to volunteer to test the clarity of your information. Rehearse your verbal explanation and ask them to check that your information sheet would offer them the reassurances they would want.

Equalities

If the broad purpose of service evaluation is to improve outcomes for the end user and to seek to sustain high-quality projects that bring benefits to individuals and communities, that will necessarily involve efforts to think about the nature of our clientele and to find out whether or not the full range of their different needs is met. It becomes a matter of justice to take every possible step to ensure that our methods do not mean a particular group of service users is overlooked or excluded from offering their views, because if that happens our evaluation can perpetuate inequalities in our services. This may well be unintentional but such issues can easily be glossed over in our sampling, methods or analysis.

The issue of sampling is further addressed in Chapter 7. It is sufficient to say here that the choice of how to select your sample can be affected by equalities issues. A random sample of, say, every tenth user might be statistically representative. If, however, you know that 30 per cent of the project's clients belong to the Muslim faith, it might be necessary to use a 'stratified sample', which selects people randomly within their faith group and in proportion to the numbers of that group in the user population. Otherwise, the sample may insufficiently reflect the views and needs of Muslim users. Sometimes you will be aware that it is crucial to make sure that the views of certain groups are included in your evaluation, (such as patients with particular conditions), and the evaluator will therefore select a quota on a 'non-random basis' to ensure that, however small they are, those groups are included.

Our methods need careful examination for each situation. Postal questionnaires, for example, will exclude people who cannot read. Even those with generally poor literacy skills may find them too threatening and many people will not even open the envelope. The same may apply to clients who have a chaotic life style or are afraid of officialdom. Language needs to be simple enough for everybody to understand, or support should be offered: a respondent who is deaf may need a sign language interpreter or might find it easier to respond on a computer. People whose first language is not English may need an interpreter, or questionnaires may need to be translated. Sometimes the nature of our questions or the way in which the interviewer is dressed may be unacceptable in certain minority communities. In many situations, it is also preferable to have an interviewer of the same sex as the respondent. Returning to our example above, if the researcher only schedules interviews on Friday afternoons, this may exclude many Muslim families who will be attending the mosque. High non-response rates are often a signal that the methods of the evaluation have excluded certain groups so to get the best response in future, we may need to adapt our choice of methods. It is good practice to pilot our intended methods with members of those excluded groups about whom we have concerns or to find someone with expert knowledge of their situation to advise us.

Our proposals for analysing the findings need a similar reality-check. If a particular group may have specific needs or suffer exclusion in some way, we need to collect information that enables us to analyse that as a factor. The most common factors that influence the outcome of services in this way are social class, race, gender and disability but there are many others that play a part in disadvantage in particular situations. It will not always be appropriate but if such factors are likely to be influencing service take-up, provision or outcomes, we do need to collect information on those characteristics to enable us to examine what exactly is happening. For example, some social or racial groups have been shown to be underachieving in certain education settings when compared with other groups. It is too late, for instance, in an evaluation of a educational project to realise at the writing-up stage that no demographic characteristics of users have been collected and that therefore no analysis can be made of whether underachievement is occurring or not. This leaves the report open to the legitimate criticism that key factors were overlooked and that the benefits were likely to be experienced by some users but not those in other significant groups.

Green and South (2006) argue that in the context of health provision evaluation needs to consider not only whether the users of a service have benefited but also the issues of the reach of the service and how easy it is to access it (pp.113–128). Hidden communities or those who are 'hard to reach' may have health needs but not be aware of the services available or may find them unfriendly and difficult to use. Evidence, however good, that those who do use the service have experienced health improvements still begs the question of those whose needs were not met. This principle applies to most other service provision in other fields, where the spread or style of the service may not be sufficient to meet the needs of particular groups. The evaluator can help to address this potential gap in the evidence by using monitoring information on usage and demographic characteristics of users and employing appropriate additional methods to capture the views and needs of non-users and groups that may be excluded. Such strategies might include adapting language or evaluation tools; involving users from the vulnerable groups as respondents or peer researchers; or working through those practitioners and local community leaders who know the groups in question well.

Practice example

The Shared Care Solihull Programme is managed by The Children's Society. It works with children and young people with disabilities or complex needs. As part of the 'Ask Us' project, the staff and young people have contributed to materials and resource packs to assist workers who want to improve their practice with disabled young people.

In the Ask Us research on strategic planning, interviewers met with a number of young people to discuss their needs and their involvement in planning of services, whatever that might be. As part of the resource material, a DVD is available on the lessons learned. These are just as applicable to evaluation activity with any age group of people with specific needs as they are to research projects with children and young people. The researchers found that most of the young people could not understand the concepts of strategic planning and could not give direct responses to their questions. However, they *'could and did communicate… and did talk about school, family, their social life… their feelings'* in ways that could inform the research.

The young people and those who interviewed them made the point that *'whilst working with profoundly disabled young people, some of whom use augmentative communication systems, you have to remember that it takes time, patience, planning and an understanding of the way the young people communicate.'* This might include the use of body language, facial expressions, eye pointing, drawing or writing.

Time and patience are critical. Communication can be very different from our usual hasty social interactions. Interviewing cannot be done quickly or alongside something else: it may be necessary to meet on several occasions or to ask the same question more than once. Some forms of communication, such as inputting onto a computer that simulates speech, may be extremely slow depending on the nature of the disability. It is important not to give up and not to resort to guessing what people are saying. Communication should be considered in a variety of formats, depending on the needs concerned. These may include Braille, symbolic languages such as Widgit, audio or online systems.

'Don't make assumptions …all children can and do communicate… they may do it differently. The way forward is that profoundly disabled children and young people do make choices and will be part of strategic planning. Ask us!'

Resources from the Ask Us project are available from The Children's Society website on http://sites.childrenssociety.org.uk/disabilitytoolkit/toolkit

In order to ensure that your evaluation design does not exclude or disadvantage any identifiable group, you should be able to give a confident and satisfactory answer to these three significant questions.

- Do I have enough information about the reach of the service and access to it, to put the outcome evidence for those who do use it into a proper context?

- Could my planned methods exclude a group or type of person from being considered or offering their views?

- Will my samples and my questions give me enough information to analyse whether groups that are known to suffer relevant disadvantage elsewhere are adequately served in the context of the work I am evaluating?

Protecting children and vulnerable adults

Child-protection principles affect every area of service delivery – virtually the same principles apply to working with vulnerable adults, whether that is on account of disability, learning difficulties, old age or physical or mental health or some other reason. These principles impinge on evaluation activities in line with the over-arching ethical principle that we must not harm those involved or cause them any detriment.

Safeguarding and child protection are one exception to the general rule of confidentiality. The other issue usually excepted is specific knowledge about a major crime that is about to happen, often taken to refer especially to acts of terrorism. These are issues that fall outside the guarantee of confidentiality. This should be made clear in the introduction to the evaluation in words that are not too frightening such as 'Remember that if you tell us that you are in danger or someone is harming or abusing you or other young people, or that you know that some serious crime is to be committed, we will have to get someone to help you and cannot keep that information to ourselves.' Many children are now familiar with such warnings from other contexts such as school. The respondent should be clearly aware that if they declare abuse, the evaluator will have no option but to pass the information on to the appropriate person dealing with child protection so that something can be done. This then provides the child with a clear choice of remaining silent on the subject or telling the evaluator if they want help. The evaluator needs to be aware of where to report any concerns that arise such as disclosures of abuse. The procedures can usually be found in your own organisation's Child Protection Policy or through your local authority.

Occasionally the evaluator will discover evidence of abuse of children or vulnerable adults not through disclosure by the victim but in some other way. Computer files, for example, might contain signs of staff use of child pornography. Physical signs of violence or certain talk amongst a peer group might raise warning signals. The same principle applies here: if you have evidence that abuse is, or could be, happening, you must pass on that evidence to the person responsible for safeguarding procedures.

As mentioned earlier, most agencies would normally recommend that the parents or carer of a child under 16 should be asked to give permission if their child is to be interviewed as part of any evaluation. This is part of reassuring parents that adults with harmful intentions do not have direct access to their child but it may also serve to highlight any issues of particular vulnerability to which the researcher needs to be sensitive. Interviewers who will be dealing with children should have had Criminal Records Bureau (CRB) checks as they are working in a position of trust. This may also apply in some situations with adults. Proof of identity should always be carried and be capable of being checked: abusers have been known to masquerade as researchers.

If it is decided that incentives will be offered to increase response rates, attention should be paid to the ethical considerations involved and to the protection of respondents. Cash payments should be avoided as these can be used for harmful things like drugs or alcohol. Tokens or goods should come from reputable companies. Any rewards given in the form of special activities should clearly be appropriate for the group in question. (e.g. in respect of ages, abilities or cultural background). Care should also be exercised so that the process to select participants is as fair as possible so that some individuals are not selected for potential reward where others in the group do not have that opportunity.

Bear in mind that for some interviewees certain questions or exercises could touch on sensitive subjects or re-awaken distressing memories. This can obviously apply to anybody who has been abused in the past but may also apply to more common issues such as bereavement or illness. It is good practice, therefore, to include both the number of a contact within the service agency and an appropriate confidential advice line in the information for respondents, so that they have somewhere to turn if they do not want to talk directly to the researcher about their feelings. With subjects such as drug or alcohol abuse or domestic violence the interviewee may then become motivated to find help for themselves or someone they know. In this case they should not have to ask the researcher directly for help if they do not wish to do so but should be pointed to relevant sources of support in the evaluation information.

The evaluator should also take care to avoid any actions that could encourage perpetrators of abuse or give them access or information that they should not have. Information that is made public in the form of references to individuals in a report, or in film or photographs, can inadvertently provide perpetrators of abuse with further opportunity, especially where they are searching for that individual or for a certain type of victim. The evaluator can best protect against this sort of opportunism by attending scrupulously to the principle of anonymity and seeking permission for any use of details or images where there might be any doubt. All filming and photographic displays carry risks: an innocent picture of a school performance might for instance give an abusive former partner the clue they want about where to look for the child. The permission of the individual or parents (for under-16s) should always be sought before any photographs are used or filming is allowed at events. Online surveys and chat rooms also carry some risk of access to information by abusers. The security of the site is paramount and advice on the use of the Internet in research can be found in the ethical guidance of the major professional societies.

The evaluator in direct contact with children or vulnerable adults should be aware of how their activities appear in relation to safeguarding issues. It is generally advisable to interview children either in a public place or with another adult present so as to minimise the likelihood of misunderstanding or accusations of inappropriate behaviour. Likewise, physical contact should be kept to a minimum and used with caution. Intrusive personal questions should be reviewed to ensure that they are absolutely necessary and it should always be made crystal clear that the interviewee has the option to decline to answer. Where the respondent is vulnerable, it is especially important to avoid any suggestion of pressure to take part in the evaluation or to answer particular questions. Occasionally a teacher, social worker or carer in *loco parentis* will need to give permission for a child or vulnerable adult to be involved in an evaluation if they have difficulties in understanding such processes. This is all the more reason for taking careful steps to help the respondent give their own proper consent with as much understanding as possible.

Legal constraints

The fact of their observing ethical codes does not put researchers or evaluators beyond the law. There may be fascinating questions in areas such as criminal behaviour or racist attitudes that could be investigated in ways that would involve breaking the law. This cannot be justified and should never be considered in evaluation activities.

The Data Protection Act 1998 is the subject of many useful guidelines available on the Internet (for example, Information Commissioner's Office 2009). Most large agencies will have a data protection policy and sometimes a named officer responsible. The Act sets out provisions intended to prevent the misuse of personal data. These mean that data about individuals must be stored securely and that the information must only be used to further the purpose for which it was originally given. Mailing lists, for example, cannot be passed on to external evaluators for the purpose of mailing out questionnaires because the contact details were not given for that purpose. In that case it would be necessary for the agency concerned to write to the service users on their list asking them to agree to such a use (or as is more common, to opt out if they would be unhappy with such a use). Evaluators should be extremely careful about taking documents, laptops or disks anywhere outside their own premises if there is any risk of loss or theft of personal data. In some cases, such as inspection of case files, the agency concerned may require the evaluator to work on the material on site so that there is no transfer of data or risk of loss. You can help to make sure you stay within the law about data protection by:

- collecting only that information you really need
- keeping it no longer than is necessary
- ensuring that only the team directly involved have access to it
- reporting details anonymously
- keeping documents in secure storage.

The law does not provide evaluators with any special privileges. While confidentiality should normally be respected (and in any case, most of the detailed information relating to individuals is of no particular interest beyond informing the findings of the report), nevertheless there can be circumstances where there is a legal duty to disclose some information. The need to prevent abuse of the respondent or imminent danger to themselves or others overrides the considerations of confidentiality and anonymity here, particularly as we have explained above in matters of child abuse or self-harm.

What do you do if your results reveal problems?

The final ethical issue on which we want to touch is that which arises when the evaluation shows up significant problems in the organisation under consideration. Problems such as child protection, fraud or criminality have already been mentioned. Wider and more subtle problems can be caused by results that are unfavourable to the organisation in relation to outcomes and methods of work. Not infrequently such findings will give rise to pressure on the evaluators to amend their conclusions. If it is known at the very start of discussions that this is likely to happen, that the evaluators will not be able to report their findings accurately and that the report will be compromised, then it may be prudent to decline the work in the first place (especially if you are an external evaluator). A weak report will not help the organisation and will probably be ignored: it may not be an ethical use of resources.

Some amendments of tone or emphasis may be perfectly legitimate but not those that fundamentally jeopardise the integrity of the study. Where such pressure is considerable and the evaluator has the sense that a line must be drawn, these points may be helpful to the negotiation.

- Be sure that it is genuinely possible to say that the results have been double-checked for accuracy.

- Emphasise to the organisation that credibility is increased by showing that the agency is open to criticism and has changed work practices as a result. Negative findings are not always negative for a responsive organisation in the long term. An account of a perfect programme does not make credible reading: evidence, on the other hand, of an organisation using formative evaluation well, does.

- Offer to draw out particular positives such as other outcomes achieved that were not necessarily part of the original scheme, or strengths developed in the skills of staff.

- Ensure that the particular measures taken, the sample and the methods used are clearly shown so that readers can judge for themselves whether the evaluation design itself has in any way contributed to less than positive findings.

In the end, the report belongs to the organisation that commissioned it. It does not normally belong to the evaluator, whether internal or external, in the manner of personal research. It is essential to clarify such issues of ownership at the setting up stage and to have some idea how the report is likely to be disseminated. Often the organisation concerned can, if it chooses, refuse to publish or submit the findings. It is preferable to see that happen than to sacrifice the integrity of the evaluation itself. If we operate ethically, our respect for the service users and the need to be honest with them mean that we must be true to our findings. The potential damage to clients of fudging issues of bad practice is too great to be countenanced.

CHAPTER 6

What Do I Need to Know to Answer the Key Evaluation Questions?

In Chapter 4, we suggested some crucial matters to be decided in formulating a plan for an evaluation. These included: deciding the reasons why the evaluation is needed; identifying the outcomes the intervention hopes to achieve and considering the indicators that might show evidence of those outcomes. In this chapter, we will be chiefly addressing the question of how to choose indicators or measures that link to the outcomes you have claimed so that you are in a position to collect some evidence about them. We also discuss the question of how to make sure your evidence on those measures has maximum credibility.

Clarifying the research questions

The first step is to clarify the central evaluation questions. That involves returning to the rationale for the evaluation and the questions that need to be answered. Whatever else is an issue, what we are arguing in this book is that your organisation will need evidence of the benefits of its work. You will probably already have worked at identifying these outcomes and now have a list to hand. If not, it is a good idea to go back and give some more thought to the section in Chapter 3 on identifying outcomes. For each outcome your project claims, your evaluation will need to seek out some evidence on whether or not this has been achieved.

This will, then, provide you with a simple list of questions to be addressed. Was the first outcome achieved or not? Similarly, was the second outcome achieved and so on? Beyond that there may be other evaluation questions, such as those about the methods used, service improvement or value for money that we discussed in Chapter 1. When you have listed all these questions, the next stage is to ask yourself what information you could possibly gather to provide some evidence to answer them. Try not to plunge into gathering material or talking to people until you are quite sure what questions you are trying to answer and what evidence you need. Work through the steps methodically. You will find it pays off as when you come to report writing it will be much easier to structure your report and arrange the information you have collected.

What do 'data' and 'evidence' mean?

The terms 'data' and 'evidence' crop up so much in the discussion of evaluating outcomes that it is appropriate to pause here briefly to ensure a common understanding of how they are used. Looking in a dictionary we find that:

- *Evidence* means 'the available facts or circumstances, supporting or otherwise a belief or proposition or indicating whether or not a thing is true or valid'.
- *Data* means 'known facts or things used as a basis for inference or reckoning'. (Tulloch 1996)

The dictionary does not provide the most imaginative of reading so we will take an analogy here. Think of a fictional detective like Sherlock Holmes or, if you have more modern inclinations, try the Crime Scene Investigation (CSI) television series. Sherlock Holmes collected 'data': it was the facts, the witness testimony, the physical signs he noticed that told him the story of what had happened. He based his conclusions not on hunches but on the evidence that demonstrated who had committed each dastardly murder. Holmes approved of gathering data to solve the crime and despised anything less than an account with real evidence behind it. Forensic science has obviously moved on since that era but the principles remain the same. In today's equivalent such things as fingerprints, tyre marks, blood samples, DNA, ballistics or even flower pollen are collected by scenes of crime officers and carefully stored away in evidence bags, together with all the documents such as witness statements, photographs, or mobile phone records. The data that supports the belief about guilt is used in court and can also be challenged on the basis of any other data that presents a contrary view. If there is insufficient evidence, if the facts will not support a conviction, then it is unlikely that charges will be brought.

Of course, the data for your evaluation will not come from scenes of crime officers or crime databases. The data will be the facts you collect yourself. They will tell you about the inputs, activities, outputs and outcomes of your project or service.

Data falls into two categories:

- *Quantitative* data is that which you can count, measure or quantify; it shows numbers of things, proportions, percentages and statistics.

- *Qualitative* data is concerned with how people understand what is going on, what meanings they give to things and how they behave. It is often narrative but it can also be visual images and pictures. It tells a story that reveals depth and richness; it tells us about perceptions, feelings and qualities. Qualitative data can also be subjected to 'quantitative analysis', for example, by counting the opinions of a client group to show that 75 per cent of them said they felt healthier after the programme.

Many evaluation reports use both sorts of data as evidence.

It is important to think imaginatively about the information you already have or might be able to collect. Yet another survey is not always the best way of showing your successes. There may be data available from a number of different sources, and we will deal with potential sources of information and methods for data-gathering later on in Chapter 7.

As an evaluator, you are the detective. The outcomes claimed may or may not have been achieved. You need to collect data, use your 'forensic' skills, and decide what the evidence tells you. You are looking for more than just one or two heart-warming stories. You are looking for the facts that will 'support or otherwise' a belief that the outcomes were achieved or partially achieved. Your report has to convince other people about your conclusions.

What evidence do I need?

The evidence you need will necessarily be related to the outcomes set for the project or service you are considering, together with any facts that will answer any additional questions required (such as value for money or management issues). You must be able to link the evidence you collect to the original outcomes. Otherwise, you will end up with a mass of potentially interesting facts that are irrelevant to the main question of whether or not the outcomes were achieved.

There is an infinite list of what might be collected as the data can be about anything at all. In a project about offenders, for instance, one could collect data on their numbers of offences after involvement but, for the sake of argument, one could also collect information on the professions (if any) of their parents or what they liked to eat or the size of their shoes. It is easy to see, however, that some information is likely to be nonsense and of no value. We, therefore, need to decide what is relevant to the question we are trying to answer. If we have no knowledge or theory about the relationship of an offender's shoe size to their pattern of crime, then those facts are just irrelevant 'noise' in this context. We need to select those items of information for collection that can best be used as a 'basis for inference' about how far the outcomes were achieved. It is wise practice to try to select the smallest amount of data to collect that will address the key questions. Sheer quantities of data will not help you: unless you know how this can answer your questions it is more than likely that it will just sit unused in a filing cabinet.

These matters are best addressed at the very beginning of a piece of work rather than, as is usually the case, when the evaluation is about to start. To do this, a systematic list needs to be made:

- What are the intended outcomes for this project?
- What indicators could tell us about those outcomes?
- What information are we therefore choosing to collect?

Indicators and measures

The choice of indicators is a critical part of evaluating outcomes. As we explained earlier, outcomes do not usually come with pre-defined measures: we may have to choose what indicators we will use to say whether or not the outcome is achieved. Indicators are 'proxy measures' – for something you cannot measure directly, you find an indicator that tells you about it and gives you some reasonable measurement.

We have found the analogy of illness and symptoms helpful to understanding what an indicator means. Think about the signs of illness or of getting well again. How does a parent know that their child has chickenpox? How do they know when the child is on the mend? They cannot directly see the virus. They see the symptoms instead. The most obvious sign would be the rash, but there will probably be other symptoms such as nausea, fever, headache or loss of appetite. The signs of recovery could start with a return to a normal temperature, increased appetite, more energy and less itching: the crusts on the blisters will eventually dry up and fall off. These are the things we look for using our basic knowledge and common sense: they are also 'indicators'.

All good indicators resonate with common sense. They should not be abstract or theoretical but should be recognisable to an untrained lay person as something that shows evidence of the change in question. They may have a more complex measure or statistic behind them but the indicator should make sense as a statement of the change that can be observed.

Choosing indicators involves picturing the situation (the outcomes) you hope to achieve. Friedman (2005) suggests that you should ask yourself these three questions:

- What would it look like if we achieved it?

- How will we know we've got there?

- What will the new situation be like when we experience it?

If you get stuck, he also suggests trying the question, 'If your service was terrible, how would it show up in the lives of your customers?' (pp.54–56 and pp.165–166).

Whatever the focus of your work, you can apply these questions to help you select your indicators. For each outcome, jot down all the things you can imagine changing. What would it look like in concrete terms that a local person or a service client could recognise? These are the potential indicators.

Let us take an example of a team of neighbourhood wardens setting out to make an estate cleaner and safer for its residents. The local people could easily say what a cleaner and safer neighbourhood would look like for them. In practical terms, there might be less graffiti on the doors and walls of the local shops; there might be less litter and less flytipping; there might be fewer 'muggings' or street robberies; there might be fewer calls to the police about anti-social behaviour; there might be less evidence that drug users have been 'shooting up' or sniffing glue on the stairways of the flats; parents might be more willing to let their children play in the park; elderly people might be feeling less afraid. All those factors could be indicators: you could collect evidence about whether they had changed or not.

Taking another example, many projects would argue that their users gain in confidence in some way. Measuring that gain or capturing evidence for it is, however, rather harder. A key step is choosing indicators that make sense in the context. Ask yourself how an ordinary observer would know that a young mother, a workplace trainee or a school pupil had gained in confidence and self-esteem. The symptoms (or indicators) could, for instance, be the ability to talk to other people, ability to mix with new people, willingness to try out new experiences, physical demeanour, making eye contact (though it should be noted that this is not acceptable in all cultures), being prepared to speak in public, not being embarrassed to ask for explanations or help, the ability to say 'no' to pressure from others, and so on. You can probably add to the list yourself. Data could be gathered on any of these factors, either from the users themselves or from those who know them well, or by observation.

Practice example

Tutors who work with learners of any age know how much they gain from the process of learning, in addition to the certificate they obtain at the end of the programme. Learners often increase in confidence as a key benefit.

In 2003, NIACE (National Institute of Adult Continuing Education) undertook a small-scale research project on the significance of changes in confidence among learners and the impact on them. In 2004, the research tools were further developed for use in a teaching situation. Catching Confidence tools in a variety of formats were devised by a range of adult-learning providers and their students. The purpose was to use them to identify learning strategies that consciously develop confidence and to find ways of recording the outcomes. This had direct relevance to recognising and recording progress potentially in all forms of education but especially in informal education, where learning is not certificated by an awarding body.

Around the same time the Youth Affairs Unit at De Montfort University ran an action-research project involving youth workers and young people in a similar process. Here groups were trialling the research tools used in the national Evaluation of the Impact of Youth Work (Merton *et al.* 2004) and customising them to capture the evidence of outcomes in their own work. In both projects the process was found to be valuable for the recipients of the service (adult learners or young people); the staff (tutors or youth workers); and wider stakeholders (such as learning providers and managers of Youth Services).

The indicators of confidence used for young people included the following:

> *I am confident* ....to speak in a group; ...with adults; ...asking for help; ...meeting new people; ...saying what I feel; ...in situations which might be difficult; ...that I can affect some things in my life; ...I can bounce back when down.

Having identified appropriate indicators, one way of gathering data is to ask the respondents to rate themselves on each indicator on a scale from 'highly confident' to 'very low confidence'. In Chapter 7, you will see how such indicators can be used in different ways to build tools to gather evidence of the changes achieved.

(Comfort *et al.* 2006;
National Institute of Adult Continuing Education 2005)

There is no single correct answer about which indicators to choose. For each outcome, there will be any number of factors that could potentially be measured to judge whether things have improved or clients have benefited. Friedman (2005) gives an example of the different indicators chosen in each of two American states to measure results on the outcome of keeping children in stable families. The outcome was almost exactly the same in both cases but the indicators chosen were different (p.54). That is not important: there is no right way to do it.

Amongst the mass of potential indicators, you should try to select:

- those that can be easily understood, that communicate well to lay people. (If you explained it to the person sitting next to you on the train, he or she would nod and say it made sense.)

- those that are the most powerful proxies for the outcome. (This means that the indicator has a powerful and telling relationship to the outcome. For example, the recorded crime rate is a powerful and generally accepted indicator of local crime. On the hypothetical estate in our example above, the crime rate, the number of complaints to the police and the number of anti-social behaviour orders would all make powerful indicators for whether or not the sense of safety on the estate was improving or not.)

- those that have reliable data about them readily available or that can be collected without major difficulty. (Indicators should be dropped from the list where there is no data available about them or where it would be very difficult to gather it.)

You need to settle on two or three indicators at most for each outcome: more than that simply gets confusing. Make sure you deal with this issue right at the outset if at all possible and build it into your evaluation design. Keep trying to choose things that make sense to ordinary people; you don't need to be a trained statistician to understand a good indicator. And make sure that the ones you choose *can* be measured in some way; there's no mileage in indicators that are too difficult to measure.

After that, of course, you need to make sure that your monitoring and evaluation or information from your partners can actually record and capture these indicators. Once again, there are options about how to collect information on each indicator. If we return to our example of the neighbourhood wardens, they might well decide to use the amount of graffiti on the local shops as an indicator. In order to gather evidence about that they could ask the shopkeepers to take photographs and keep a diary of incidents. Alternatively, they could monitor the number of call-outs from the estate to the 'clean up' team, or they might ask the residents a survey question on whether they thought the amount of 'tagging' and spraying was getting better or worse. All those options would be valid measures, though the latter is perhaps less powerful as a proxy, because it depends to a greater extent on the subjective opinions of individuals. In Chapter 7, we shall develop the discussion about the range of methods that you might consider and their various advantages and disadvantages. For now, the key step is to be sure that you have your outcomes clear and that you know which indicators you will use to find out about them, with some idea of how you will gather that evidence.

Practice example

Change Support Difference (CSD) Ltd conducted an impact evaluation of Heywood Youth Inclusion Project (YIP) in the north of England, which illustrates how different measures can be gathered for a particular indicator. Heywood YIP had been operational since 2006, supported by the Heywood New Deal for Communities with some additional funding from the Youth Justice Board. It was managed by Catch22 (formerly Rainer Crime Concern). The evaluators were asked to comment on the outcomes in terms of any positive differences the project had made in its three-year life to the young people involved, their families and local stakeholders.

Youth Inclusion Projects (YIPs) were originally developed by Crime Concern in partnership with The Groundwork Trust and Marks and Spencer to engage with a core group of young people who are identified by partners as most at risk of offending and with a wider group of their peers who participate in some of the activities provided. The model has now been adopted by the Youth Justice Board to reduce youth crime and anti-social behaviour in specific neighbourhoods.

The central aim is to reduce the year-on-year reoffending of the young people recruited to the activities. The Youth Justice Board provides a specific formula for Youth Inclusion Projects whereby the indicator of offending rates of their core groups of young people can be calculated. This compares each young person's 'Standard Units of Offending' for the period from their first offence up to engagement on the YIP and then subsequently. Based on this formula, Heywood YIP was able to report a 68 per cent reduction in offending amongst its first core group and an 80 per cent reduction for its second core group.

The evaluators provided a more rounded picture by analysing other offence information on this indicator as well. They analysed the changes in the number and types of offences committed by the core group for the six months prior to their engagement and subsequently over the six months after engagement. This gives a picture of the reduction in certain types of offences (for example, from 14 offences of Violence Against the Person by the core group over the whole six-month period prior to engagement down to 5 afterwards). It also enables a closer examination of the six months immediately prior to the involvement in the project and ignores offences that happened a long time in the past. The changes over the more recent period are naturally smaller for most participants than the percentage change over the longer period since the very first offence, but the picture of the impact of the project is more accurate and convincing with this additional detail.

The report also details the other indicators of anti-social behaviour chosen and the evidence gathered for them, such as the levels of youth crime in Heywood compared with the general figures for the borough of Rochdale, where it is located, or the drop in incidents of fire-setting as supplied by the Fire and Rescue Service. The report offers a very full picture of where changes in patterns of youth offending have occurred, and illustrates well how evidence can be identified and gathered against particular indicators.

(Change Support Difference Ltd 2009, unpublished)

The indicators used need to be as accurate and descriptive as possible. They should relate clearly to outcomes. In some cases, it is possible to adjust them for the risk in each case of a poor outcome. Not all young people, for instance, present the same risk that they will offend in later life. In the example above, all the young people whose records were examined had been assessed as presenting a high risk of offending and thus could reasonably be compared.

This issue of risk is particularly clear in the medical field. Defending the accusation that 'risk-adjusted outcome measures' are just gobbledegook, Roy Maxwell FRCS wrote a deliberately understated letter to *The Times*.

> For most cancer patients, the outcome of their treatment is quite important – factors such as their chance of survival and quality of life. Outcome is affected by stage of presentation of cancer and co-existing illness, risks that must be taken into account in producing meaningful information on results of treatment. Good quality outcome measures are the most efficient means of assuring patients that the centre treating them achieves national and international standards. (*The Times* 2009)

Practice example

Risk assessment scales are frequently used to assist in nursing patients who may develop pressure ulcers. These wounds caused by immobility present huge problems. If pressure is placed on a part of the body, blood circulation is reduced. This is not a problem in healthy people as they are constantly moving, even in sleep. In an unconscious or paralysed patient if the blood supply is reduced for long enough the tissue dies and rots away. The pressure ulcer is basically a hole in the body caused by the death of good tissue from pressure damage. About one in five hospital patients develops a pressure ulcer. Often these are trivial, merely a small break in the skin, but they can be extensive with gaping holes down to the bone. They can kill.

In order to evaluate methods of preventing and treating such ulcers, it is necessary to have indicators of their severity which everybody will understand. Because some patients are more at risk than others it is also necessary to have some way of taking risks into account when comparing the outcomes for patients. Accurate indicators of risk will also help nurses to prioritise those with the greatest likelihood of developing ulcers.

Early research showed that patients who moved during sleep at least twenty times per night were less likely to develop pressure ulcers than those who moved less. Mobility was thus one factor, but in 1962 scores for several other factors, incontinence, activity, mental state and physical condition, were added to mobility to create the first pressure-ulcer risk assessment scale. In the UK, hospitals now tend to use the Waterlow score. (Waterlow 1991) This consists of eleven main sub-scores with various ranges, including the factor of being terminally ill with cancer. The sub-scores are added together to give an overall risk score.

Assessment of patients for the risk of developing pressure ulcers on admission to hospitals in the UK is now common. The idea is that if we can determine who is at high risk – because we know the indicators – we can reduce the possibility of pressure ulcers. A frail elderly patient who has a fracture of the neck of the femur (broken hip) is likely to develop an ulcer because of their immobility. A twenty-year-old admitted for removal of wisdom teeth is pretty unlikely to have this problem. So, if we have one special bed which reduces the pressure on the patient, we know which patient should have it. We may want to put other special measures in place. For example, elderly patients often have poor nutrition so we may refer the fractured hip patient to the dietician. This is especially important as poorly fed patients tend to develop pressure ulcers more quickly. A high Waterlow score shows a patient is at risk.

There are, however, problems with using this score. We might not have all the risk factors (for example, low blood protein is associated with pressure ulcers). Some of the alleged risk factors may not be a problem for some patients or may be insignificant. For example, the Waterlow score gives a higher score to women than men but women and men have roughly equal chances of getting pressure ulcers so this may not be sensible. There are problems with reliability due to the subjective nature of some of the factors, and two nurses often give very different scores for the same patient. Furthermore no study has shown that using the Waterlow score actually improves pressure ulcer incidence. Research is continuing through the School of Nursing at De Montfort University to find more accurate indicators of risk and more precise measures of severity. To be effective the factors included in risk scores must all be genuine causes of adverse outcome, all the significant factors should be included and their relative importance should be taken into account. An accurate assessment scale should reduce poor outcomes such as pressure ulcers or deep vein thrombosis. The positive outcome is the aim: assessment tools need to be sufficiently precise to make a difference to results. Those that do not change outcomes may not be an improvement on sound clinical judgement.

(Saleh, Anthony and Parboteeah 2009)

In a small project, the measures may be very simple. For example, in a schools project aiming to provide children with information about domestic violence and how they could seek help, the agency chose indicators of the knowledge and awareness of the children about domestic violence and the views of teachers in the schools concerned on the effect of the programme. They used a short quiz with the children before and after the sessions. These showed improvements in awareness of the causes and prevalence of domestic violence and a sharp increase in knowledge about how to seek help. In addition, the providers interviewed some of the teachers and obtained qualitative evidence of the ways in which they had picked up comments from the children, seen the impact on them and found an increased reporting of violence. The indicators and methods you choose need to be geared to the resources at your disposal and the context of the practice.

The 'hard' and 'soft' dilemma

Many of the differences we reckon as positive change in our lives are in fact very small and may not show up in official figures. They cannot easily be measured and counted. This has led many practitioners to fear evaluation because they feel that good outcomes are often less tangible, that their clients make slow small steps of progress that are absolutely essential but can easily be discounted in the headline statistics.

For example, in the field of assisting people to gain or re-enter employment, workers are often dealing with clients who have lost self-esteem and have a sense of rejection, have poor social skills or lack educational qualifications. For some it may be too daunting even to pick up the phone and ask for an application form. In these circumstances, there is often a long period of trying to increase job-readiness. There may be many painful steps and little victories on the way, such as learning to get up in the morning on time, having the courage to travel to another part of the city, learning to complete a form or CV, perhaps improving literacy or numeracy and, above all, building self-confidence again. Some clients may make enormous progress but still fail to secure a job. Their gains do not show up in the employment statistics at all.

This dilemma has led many evaluators to talk about 'hard' and 'soft' outcomes:

Hard outcomes

'Hard outcomes' can be measured and quantified in a definable way that avoids doubt and subjectivity. There are clearly debates about how the

Activity

Table 6.1 shows the outputs and outcomes for an imaginary project funded by a Primary Care Trust and aiming to reduce obesity for overweight adults referred by their GPs.

- Apply this example by drawing up a similar table for a project you know well. See if you can express its outcomes clearly and simply.

- Use the matrix below to list its outputs and how they are monitored.

- Then list the outcomes and suggest the indicators you might choose and how you would collect the evidence for them.

TABLE 6.1: OUTPUTS AND OUTCOMES FOR THE 'SHAPE UP WEIGHT LOSS PROGRAMME'

Project purpose: To provide weight loss, dietary advice and encouragement to exercise for adults over 45 who are registered with their GPs as obese, in order to reduce the potential for health problems such as heart disease, diabetes or high blood pressure.

Activities: (focus of the work) Weekly group meetings. Telephone support from trained weight-loss advisers. Provision of tailored weight-loss plans for individual participants.

Outputs	How are they monitored?	Outcomes (benefits for the users = the effect of the work)	Indicators (What will show the outcome has been achieved?)	Methods (How will the evidence be collected?)
Number of referrals from GP practices Number of participants registering on programme Age, gender, ethnic origin and medical conditions of participants Number of participants completing the 12-week course Attendances at group meetings Numbers of individual weight-loss plans, including diet and exercise targets agreed at start of programme with participants	Shape Up administrative staff record referrals, registrations, demographic details of participants, and completions on a database Individual details are drawn from standard referral forms Weight-loss Adviser completes form each week with attendance, and date when plan is completed and signed Administrative staff collate forms from advisers onto data base	GPs will value having a new preventative intervention for this group of patients. Some cost savings to practices	Opinions of GPs Evidence of cost savings on alternative treatments and prescription medicines	Survey of GPs on satisfaction with scheme and estimated cost savings at end of first year
		60 per cent of participants will reduce their weight by 5 per cent over the 12-week programme	Weight of participants at start and finish of programme	Advisers record weights each week. Total weight loss and original weight are entered on database
		75 per cent of those completing the course will be regularly taking 30 minutes of moderate exercise per day	Participants reporting on weekly exercise pattern	Exit evaluation form asks participants to report how many minutes of exercise taken per day for final two weeks and to rate confidence to maintain it
		75 per cent of those completing the course will feel 'very confident' that they can stick to the nutritional goals set in their agreed weight-loss plan	Participants reporting feeling able to stick to healthy diet	Opinions of participants gathered through exit evaluation forms, which rate their confidence on a four-point scale

measures are defined but once defined there is no matter of opinion involved in measuring and recording them. Like can be compared with like. A good example is the birth weight of newborn babies. There is no doubt about what the measure means and it is often involved in estimates of maternal and child health and is a good predictor of health in later life. Another example would be the commonly used educational measure of attainment as how many GCSEs were achieved at Grades A to C.

Soft outcomes

'Soft outcomes' are those aspects of progress that are seen as difficult to measure and largely subjective. They can be final outcomes (such as becoming completely comfortable with your identity) but more frequently they are seen as temporary stages of development. They would include such things as improvements in relationships, self-control, mental health, motivation and self-esteem. Sometimes the gains in 'soft outcomes' over time in relation to the situation at the start are referred to as 'distance travelled'. This often deals with personal development issues and may be a more helpful term. A guidance document on evaluating the progress of clients seeking qualifications and employment through European Social Fund projects offers helpful definitions of these terms.

- *Hard outcomes*: are 'the clearly definable and quantifiable results that show the progress a beneficiary has made towards achieving desirable outcomes by participating in a project. Typically they include obtaining a qualification, finding work or securing a place on a course. Hard outcomes are usually straightforward both to identify and to measure.'

- *Soft outcomes*: are 'those outcomes that represent intermediary stages on the way to achieving a hard outcome. They could include, for example, thinking skills such as improved problem-solving abilities, personal attributes such as improved self-confidence, or practical work-focused skills, such as a better appreciation of the importance of time-keeping in the workplace. As such, it can be more difficult to define or measure them – although they may be the main outcomes achieved by the most disadvantaged … groups.'

- *Distance travelled*: 'refers to the progress beneficiaries make in achieving soft outcomes that lead towards sustained employment or associated hard outcomes, as a result of participating in a project and against an initial baseline set on joining it. By definition, measuring distance travelled will require assessing clients on two

or more separate occasions to understand what has been achieved.'
(Department for Work and Pensions and Welsh European Funding
Office 2003)

Outcomes tend to be described as 'distance travelled' or as 'soft' not because
they are easy to achieve but because they are difficult to define and measure.
They are often the steps on the way to achieving 'hard' outcomes. Although
these achievements may seem small, they are often the changes that we
observe in clients that make our work seem worthwhile. It might, for
instance, encourage us simply to see a profoundly depressed client make eye
contact and smile. Soft outcomes can, of course, be ends in themselves and
are valuable as such. We just need to recognise that the differences we are
funded to make happen at different levels.

'Soft' outcomes are not always to do with individual progress. They
can apply to organisations and communities. Green and South (2006,
pp.130–141) make the point in relation to public health practice that
many of the conditions we value for our clients and seek to promote in
our organisations are by their very nature hard to measure precisely. These
conditions would include, for instance, the participation of staff and patients,
community involvement, empowerment, a positive climate for diversity,
and good communication. Very often partnership organisations would be
expected, both by government and the public, to promote such qualities in
their relationships with their client communities. These 'fuzzy aspects' also
occur in many other fields such as community safety, education, social work,
or democratic involvement. Progress on outcomes of this type is very often
assessed by means of frameworks or scales, often using several dimensions
of the concept that can be used to assess the state of the organisation or
partnership group. The National Youth Agency 'Hear by Right' framework
(which enables services to rate their progress on defined standards in
involving young people in decision-making and active democracy) is
one such example (Badham and Wade 2005). For an agency to progress
in its own assessment like this is, in our terms, a 'soft' outcome for that
organisation.

Increasingly we, the authors, feel that the lines between hard and
soft outcomes and distance travelled are becoming blurred and that the
distinctions are in fact unhelpful. However, they are terms in common use
and they do draw attention to the need to look at the many steps involved
in achieving a final measurable result. A person might gain new motivation,
learn to read better as a means to employment and subsequently find a job,
clear their debts and improve relationships with their family as a result.
Hard (and clearly measurable) outcomes are interwoven here with those

that are less easily defined. It is impossible to say what might be the most significant outcome in this person's view and when it might occur along their journey. It is clearly nonsense to say that entry to employment is the only outcome to be valued here, though conventionally it would appear as the most commonly collected 'hard' outcome in this scenario. Outcomes pop up in all shapes and sizes and at different stages. There is no reason to discount 'soft outcomes' but outcome models would still demand that evaluation takes place to see if the changes intended, however small, are actually taking place.

Economic evaluation and the 'value for money' question

Sometimes services and projects need to provide evidence of their value for money. This is a perfectly legitimate requirement as policy-makers and commissioners are frequently in the position of having to decide where to allocate money amongst a menu of possible programmes in order to achieve particular outcomes. Clearly they need to know that a programme *does* produce the desired outcomes but there may also be choices between programmes that can *all* claim to produce those benefits. Programmes may even be using virtually identical methods and processes. Funders will naturally be asking:

- Is the work effective, and therefore likely to be worth investment?
- Is the work preventive of greater future spending?
- Could similar work be carried out at a lower price?
- Can any savings be made in this programme?

In this situation questions have to be asked about value for money or the relative efficiency of the programmes. If four similar parenting programmes show similar results in changes to family behaviour, it is likely that their costs will be compared. If one programme takes twenty weeks instead of twelve and costs twice as much per family to run, it is not likely to be the preferred choice unless it can show other added benefits. If another programme has a top-heavy structure and massive management overheads that drive up the costs, then it will also be more carefully scrutinised. The government spends billions of pounds on programmes, for instance, to reduce recidivism amongst offenders, to improve skills in the workforce, to prevent homelessness or to improve the outcomes of cancer treatment. Taxpayers' money ought not to be wasted on programmes that are much more expensive than others for the same dividend in clients' lives.

Such economic analysis is a complex area and there are many debates about how it should be properly conducted. Data on costs, both direct and indirect, needs to be gathered for the programme itself as comprehensively as possible. This includes such items as salaries, premises costs, activity and equipment costs, maintenance, management, administrative support, and so on. The annual budget is a help but it may not include everything, such as the hidden costs of in-kind support, management or volunteer time. Figures will also have to be collected to estimate comparative costs from other similar programmes. This is almost always a major problem with questions about access to accounts of other agencies and of the validity of the comparisons (see Rossi, Lipsey and Freeman 2004, pp.331–368 for detailed examples). Most projects will need expert help if value for money is a key component of their evaluation. Whether you bring in outside expertise or not, it is useful to keep any well-researched reports on costs in similar services as these may make a reference point for basic comparisons.

Certain typical measures are used to ascertain value for money:

- *Cost-effectiveness analysis* equates the outcomes of the programme to an estimated figure for the savings for services. The analysis examines whether the cost per outcome in the programme is greater or less than the theoretical savings if the outcome were not achieved. It is possible, for instance, to estimate the cost to services of criminal offences or of treatment for a particular health problem.

- *Cost-benefit analysis* estimates the benefits of a programme and the cost of undertaking the programme and calculates a financial cost per unit of benefit achieved. The project costs divided by the project benefits will give a cost–benefit ratio. The cost–benefit is the value in monetary terms of the benefits less the total cost involved in achieving them. Such calculations are naturally easier if the decision is about a business decision such as buying a new photocopier than about complex programmes dealing with people.

Unit cost calculations are sometimes attempted. Drawn from the industry model of the cost of a standard unit supplied (or output), these measures can be highly problematic as the estimated costs may be inaccurate or like may not be compared with like in terms of the actual service delivered. In the worst examples, costs may be compared, for instance, of individual, highly intensive provision such as counselling with larger scale provision for group activities. Even if costs are higher for the more intensive service, the multiple problems faced by some clients and the time required to deal them will mean a corresponding difficulty in producing outputs and outcomes in quantity and may well justify more costly services. The wider social benefits that may accrue to families or to the community are also extremely hard to value in monetary terms. There are some quite sophisticated models for estimating the return on investment in the cost of the social benefits that accrue from a project (e.g. Lawlor, Neitzert and Nicholls 2008) and it is good practice to collect evidence of savings to other services and the estimated costs of social problems. Smaller projects without specialist help will, however, usually be better placed to offer a simple cost-effectiveness analysis.

Despite the difficulties, it is always worthwhile asking basic questions about the efficiency and value of your organisation (Ellis 2005, pp.71–72). Are the resources you use the most appropriate and justifiable in terms of price? Are there any ways of making savings without reducing the positive outcomes of the work? Is the design of the project the most efficient for achieving the benefits to the users, or would other methods work better? Is the project effective in terms of its overall cost compared with the benefits it can evidence?

Practice example

In the evaluation of Heywood Youth Inclusion Project (to which we have already referred) the evaluators were asked to provide some evidence on value for money. CSD Ltd reported on several different cost-effectiveness measures to provide an estimate of the financial benefit of the service in its work of diverting young people at risk from crime.

- The Home Office research on the costs of crime (Brand and Price 2000; Dubourg, Hamed and Thorns 2005) was used to offer an estimated cost for various types of offence, and a factor for inflation was added. Building on the local crime figures for the age group, the costs of crime in Heywood and in the wider borough of Rochdale were then compared. On this measure, reductions in offending were evidenced in Heywood of 42 per cent from 2005/6 to 2007/8 in a population of 1,284 with a 'saving' of over £102,000 in economic and social costs, while in the borough as a whole the volume of crime had only reduced by 2 per cent in a population of 24,304 over the same period and costs had actually risen by £790,000.

- On the same basis, the costs of the actual crimes committed by the young people who participated in the project were compared with the costs of offences committed by those who were identified as meeting the 'at risk' criteria and referred to the project but who declined to take part. The benefits here are more likely to be directly related to the project interventions. The costs of crime committed after the period of intervention compared with the rates previously dropped significantly for those who were engaged in the project (- £290,265) while for those who did not participate, offences and costs rose (+ £12,786) over the same period and continued to escalate in the subsequent months.

- The costs of various court sentences in relation to the staff time required were supplied by the local Youth Offending Service. For example, a Referral Order was estimated to cost £567 to carry out and an Intensive Supervision Order could cost £7,388. Costs of orders in relation to the participating group had reduced, while they had escalated for the group who were referred but did not become engaged.

- Based on the research by New Philanthropy Capital, costs were also estimated for the effect of truancy and exclusion (Brookes, Goodall and Heady 2007). This report estimates the direct cost of a school exclusion (£881) and the 'whole life' costs of the effect on services (at a shocking £63,851). The Youth Inclusion Project had succeeded in returning six young people to school with obvious savings to services.

As might be expected cost benefits in financial terms are more difficult to pin down. The evaluators also offered a unit cost of engaging a young person in the YIP compared with the economic and social costs demonstrated by the non-engaged group. Costs for such intensive provision with a relatively small group are naturally considerable. A small saving on cash costs was shown but this could not take account of the wider questions of benefits to the individual in education, health and broader life chances or the gains for the community of reduced offending by local young people.

(Change Support Difference Ltd 2009, unpublished)

The credibility of the evidence

Once you have decided upon your indicators and gathered your evidence you have to test what the information is telling you. In Chapter 9 we offer some pointers on how to analyse your data. Once that analysis is complete the evaluator needs to stand back and weigh up what the evidence is saying, without siding with any of the partners concerned. If the indicators were well drafted this should not be too problematic. If an indicator is only partially met or the evidence is inconclusive, then you should say so. Returning to our analogy of the detective, this is the question of whether your evidence will stand up in court. It is not a matter of belief in your project or of sympathy for the client's needs: it is a matter of the weight and credibility of the evidence on whether the outcomes were achieved or not. There are three issues in particular that relate to whether or not your evidence will be credible.

Sampling

The nature of our sample as well as its size – how we selected the people, agencies or documents in order to seek the information we need – is fundamental to how valid the results will be. It is unlikely that we will be able to obtain feedback from all our users and stakeholders. In most circumstances, evaluators have to decide who to ask, whose views to take into account and how many people to approach. Not only is the *number* of people from whom we gain information important but so is *how we go about selecting them*. The nature of the sample is therefore, a key evaluation question.

The way in which we select our respondents affects how representative our findings will be: that is, how far our findings can be generalised as being typical of all our users. There are rules about what constitutes a valid sample if you wish to derive statistical measures from it, but even if your evaluation is not aspiring to statistical measures you should aim for it to be as representative as possible. The more rigorous our sampling methods, and (usually) the larger the sample, the more we can feel confident about our findings. From a true 'random sample' of sufficient size, it is possible to draw statistical conclusions and make generalisations about the applicability of the results to all our users.

Whatever method you use to select people it is useful to ask yourself how inclusive of a broad range of respondents is this approach? How typical are these people of the whole group under study? As described in Chapter 5, the credibility of your results will be affected by how genuinely and inclusively your sample reflects different types of users or respondents.

The central issue for the credibility of your findings is that you should be deliberate about how you select people and open in your report about how you went about it. It is crucial to explain the size of your sample and how it was selected. It is important not to exaggerate claims that can be made from the findings. The numbers of people who responded and did not respond also affect how representative the findings are and should therefore be detailed in a report. Chapter 7 describes in more detail how to go about sampling, and Chapter 9 provides further advice on how to present your results.

Triangulation

The use of this word in relation to research is drawn from the work of engineers using both horizontal and vertical angles to ensure accurate measurements of heights or distances. We see this at work in our streets when construction workers use a theodolite. They are measuring from different angles to ensure an accurate result. In evaluation this can mean using the different perspectives of several of the people concerned in the situation, or it can mean using several data-collection methods to look at the questions in different ways.

Triangulation is one of the best routes to improving the credibility of your findings. We have recommended using both qualitative and quantitative methods partly for this reason. Using varied methods, you can reinforce the findings of, say, a quantitative survey with qualitative interviews that provide detailed quotations around how the users perceived the project and how they describe their outcomes. In terms of using different angles on individuals, it can be very telling to see the participant's opinion on the changes they believe they have achieved backed up by evidence from other people such as their parents, friends or teachers. If you can obtain such triangulated evidence it will strengthen the weight of your findings considerably.

Appropriate use of numerical data

We all know the saying often attributed (without any certainty) to Disraeli about the three kinds of lies – 'lies, damn lies and statistics'. This view of statistics is so embedded in popular consciousness that many people will question any figures in official reports and how they were arrived at. However, you will need to use some numbers and statistics in your evaluation reports. There are several useful pointers to increasing their credibility for the reader.

Your aim should be to make as clear to the reader as possible what your findings actually mean. This will involve providing enough detail to avoid any ambiguity. Typical mistakes in reporting evidence include the following issues.

- *Exaggerating numbers or responses.* Percentages, for instance, can be used in a way that exaggerates numbers, when the total number in the group is very small. For example, from a small class with 14 participants, it was reported that '93 per cent had said they had learned more about their own health during the programme'. This sounds very different from saying that 13 out of 14 students said they had learned more about their health because such a high percentage rather implies that the group was much larger than it really was.

- *Failing to identify clearly the sample used,* how it was drawn and to what time period it applies. This prevents the reader from being able to judge how representative your data was – and therefore how valid the findings may be.

- *Not making clear how many people responded or benefited* and what proportion these were of the whole. For example, if only 10 children filled in evaluation forms out of 96, it is neither sufficient nor transparent to say that all those responding had improved their diet. Best practice is to provide both the actual number and the proportion; for example, '80 children out of 120 on the project (66%) now include a portion of fruit or vegetables in their food every day'. Proportions and percentages help us understand the significance of numbers. Without them, raw numbers in the text or in a table can be hard to interpret.

- *Reporting only the positive statistics* and leaving out the negative results. This leaves the reader asking 'What about the rest?' and nursing a nagging doubt about the honesty of the reporting.

- *Using self-reported responses as precise numerical measures.* Self-reported scores are subjective and may not mean the same from one respondent to another, unless the system has been extensively tested for reliability. Many of the 'soft outcome' tools yield evidence with a similar measure of subjectivity. In these circumstances, care should be taken about aggregating the data.

Some categories of numerical data just afford a head count and so each category can be totalled. They have no particular order or rank – for instance, ethnic group classifications or whether people are employed or unemployed. These are known as 'nominal' data.

Some other numbers are in 'ranked categories'. We are very familiar, for instance, with the response scales of four or more points in questionnaires running from 'strongly agree' to 'strongly disagree' and other similar response ratings. These are known as 'ordinal' data. Here it is legitimate to say that one score is more positive than another but it is impossible to say exactly how much difference there is between one score and another. The scores people provide in their responses have a meaning in the mind of the person giving them a value but there is no guarantee that they would carry exactly the same meaning for someone else. If two people respond to a question saying they 'strongly agree', there is no way of knowing whether their views are exactly the same or not as they may interpret the term differently. Similarly if I respond to a question with a score of 10, it does not necessarily mean that this response is ten times more positive than that of someone who responds with a score of 1. So what we can do is to count responses and say, for example, that 20 per cent of the group agreed strongly with the statement. We can also group responses together. For example, we could say that '47 per cent of patients reported that the treatment had made "some improvement" or "a great deal of improvement"' or that '73 per cent rated their perception of the importance of the service as scoring 7 or more out of 10.' We can also provide the range of opinion, the 'median' or mid-point, or measures of ranking (such as the highest and lowest scores or the benefit considered most important through to the least important).

Some commentators would suggest that it is not normally legitimate, however, to try to calculate average scores from different respondents or to add scores together or otherwise use them in arithmetical calculations (for example, Denscombe 2005, p.237 and pp.252–256, and Siegel 1956, pp.23–30). There may be exceptions where research instruments using self-reported scores have been tested for their reliability but in those instances the exact scoring system provided with the questionnaire or test needs to be rigorously followed (see Chapter 8, 'Existing surveys and assessment systems').

There are several other sorts of numerical data but these need not detain us here. The main message is that care should be exercised over writing up self-reported scores. Keep it simple and do not assume that the scores are precise numbers – they are simply the subjective answers of the respondents. If you need to go further, read around the topic of different types of quantitative data in a research-methods textbook or ask for advice from someone trained in statistical analysis.

A balanced picture: Friedman's essential elements of information

As we have stressed so far, the choices about what information to collect and how it should be collected should be informed by practicality and by what would make a credible evaluation for the audience concerned, but, by now, with so many possibilities on what data you might gather, you may be wondering just how much you need to do. In his work on performance accountability, Mark Friedman suggests that for balance and maximum credibility an evaluation of outcomes should have evidence on three simple performance measure questions:

- How much did the service or programme do?
- How well did they do it?
- Is anyone better off – in both qualitative and quantitative terms?

(Friedman 2005, pp.67–85)

The question of *how much* the programme did is the issue of outputs. As we set out in the discussion of planning in Chapter 4, your evaluation design needs to include the plans for monitoring and collecting the outputs of the service. They are not outcomes: outputs can be high even though the clients may not have benefited at all. They are, however, an important part of the context. They help to portray the background of your service and the value it offers.

The question of *how well* the service or programme performed in the eyes of its clients is the question of satisfaction and value. Satisfaction is rarely a true outcome: people may enjoy an activity without experiencing any real benefit. Occasionally, however, an organisation may be setting out to improve client or public perceptions and that improvement therefore constitutes an outcome in that context. Although we habitually collect more evidence on the issue of satisfaction than on outcomes, it is, in fact, a less important matter. Nonetheless, satisfaction can be an important feature of the context since users who are dissatisfied with the service will usually achieve poorer outcomes than those in a setting where there is enjoyment and few complaints – and, indeed, such views will affect the reputation of the service. If a service is unresponsive or too expensive in relation to its achievements, this will matter to those who fund it.

The crucial question is whether anybody benefited or not

Here Friedman (2005, p.67) advocates providing both qualitative and quantitative evidence. Although, classically, research designs concentrated either on quantitative methods or qualitative approaches, this no longer holds true and there are now well-established research approaches that use mixed-methods designs (Cresswell and Plano Clark 2007). The advantage of using mixed methods for evaluation at basic project level is that while you do require some facts and figures of successful outcomes (the quantitative evidence), the qualitative evidence will often help to explain to the reader the quality and depth of your work and the real nature of client needs in your service. It is very hard to gather this detailed feel of the situation from tables and graphs, and without it your report may not convey the essence of your work – especially where your clients suffer multiple needs or are severely at risk and their outcomes take pain and time to achieve. In Chapter 7, you will find a case study example and other illustrations that show just how vividly qualitative evidence can bring facts and numbers to life.

The matrix in Table 6.2 adapted from Friedman's work (2005, pp.68–69) illustrates this for a hypothetical example of drug-prevention education in schools. In your own project when you are assessing whether you are gathering enough evaluation data to answer the key evaluation questions, we suggest you use the grid to check that you will have evidence to hand for each quadrant.

TABLE 6.2: FRIEDMAN'S THREE SIMPLE PERFORMANCE-MEASURE CATEGORIES
(applied to an example of drug-prevention education in schools)

How much did the service do?	How well did they do it?
For example, evidence of: • number of school pupils participating • number of sessions held • total actual expenditure for the year	For example, evidence of: • reach, in terms of geographical location of schools involved, ethnicity, gender of pupils participating • satisfaction of the participants • cost per pupil • satisfaction of teachers with input • numbers of complaints
Is anyone better off?	
Qualitative	*Quantitative*
For example, evidence of: • detail of accounts of changed behaviour from pupils or teachers • quotations from individual interviews or focus groups, case studies, testimonials	Evidence of the proportion or percentage of those who reported successful outcomes, i.e. were 'better off'. For example: • percentage showing positive movement on scaled questions on attitudes to use of illegal drugs • proportion reporting increased self-confidence in resisting risky behaviour in relation to substances • statistically significant differences in answers to knowledge questions about drugs between those who received the programme and a group who did not

CHAPTER 7

How Do I Get That Information?

In Chapter 6 we looked at the sort of information you will need in order to answer the outcome questions, including the choice of indicators and measures. We explored the need to evidence soft outcomes as well as the facts and figures about your results and discussed how to maximise the credibility of your evidence and produce a balanced picture. In this chapter we now move on to examine where you can find that information and how to choose the best methods to collect it. We continue to place a strong emphasis on the need to be practical and realistic in your plans.

Sources of evaluation data

Once you know what information you need in order to answer your main evaluation issues and to provide measures of performance against the outcomes in question, you can start deciding where and how to gather that data. It is important not to ignore material you have already to hand in your agency. Typically, in the evaluation of projects dealing with people, the information can be gathered from these main sources.

Existing information

- To help *show the need or the context for the scheme*, you might, for instance, be able to use the original project proposal, census data, demographic data (such as the age profile or the numbers of minority ethnic groups in the population), audits of need, media stories, crime figures or service statistics.

- To describe *what the scheme provided and who it reached*, you might use minutes of meetings, programme publicity leaflets, membership information, attendance records, demographic details of participants, accreditation records, photographs or press stories.

- To help *assess overall results*, you might draw on public records such as local employment figures, public health reports, crime or anti-social behaviour statistics, school attendance data, educational achievement information, inspection reports for individual services or Joint Area Reviews, or evaluations of similar programmes.

- To help *show progress of clients as individuals*, you might draw on case files, service databases, or session records from relevant workers.

People

Your main questions are likely to be about outcomes so you need to think about who will be best placed to tell you what difference the project has made. You might consider:

- the clients or participants who receive the service or take part in the project

- their friends, parents or carers, partners, and so on who can talk about the changes that have occurred

- the paid workers who provide the service and understand its methods (including administrative and ancillary staff)

- volunteers

- key informants: people who have particular knowledge about the scheme, the problems it addresses or how it benefits participants

- 'stakeholders': people who have some interest in the scheme – perhaps as partners, as sources of referrals or as indirect clients of the service (such as schools)

- those who do not take part, or critics of your scheme

- people with certain characteristics or problems, e.g. people who have become homeless; people with specific disabilities

- people with particular expertise, such as historians, psychologists, criminologists

- residents and community leaders

- competitors or similar schemes

- funders
- local or central government managers and policy-makers.

Pictorial or audio-visual records and observations

Visual or audio-visual material may in some circumstances be more powerful than the written word. Observation can provide neutral information about what is happening. Examples might include:

- before and after photographs (e.g. the allotment project, the refurbished youth centre or local housing before and after the regeneration scheme)
- art work that shows the client's perception of their problems or the progress they feel they have made
- a CD of a group in action or the views of participants
- video material showing learning taking place with development over time, e.g. learning a language or sports skill
- observation to record the characteristics, interactions or skill development of clients or patients (e.g. people with disabilities learning to use new communication skills)
- observation of verbal and non-verbal reactions.

Ways of using the information to test and demonstrate outcomes

In Chapter 6 we discussed how we collect evidence to answer the questions about whether or not particular outcomes have been achieved and the need to test that evidence to see whether it 'will stand up in court'. The concept of outcomes is about change, difference, direction. The evidence must therefore be about change – whether that is for an individual, a group or community. A shift has occurred over a particular period – from Time 1 to Time 2 as logic models would put it.

You are therefore looking to present evidence of that change or benefit over time. The information you collect must thus be related to the period of time in question and to the activities or interventions you provided and to the difference that came about as a result. There are several basic approaches that are commonly used to demonstrate difference over time.

- *Measurement of an indicator against a baseline*
  This is often used to show changes at whole-population or group level and uses quantitative data – for example, an improvement

over time in the proportion of babies born with a low birth-weight against the baseline at a particular point, or reduction in offences for a group that received a particular form of probation support.

- *Measures or descriptions of change for individuals over a particular period of intervention – at the beginning and at the end, or before and after*
  These may be quantitative measures taken at two points in time, such as weight at the beginning and end of an obesity programme or scores on a test of children's reading ability at the start of a learning support programme and at the end. They could also be qualitative descriptions of the change conveyed, for instance, by a case study of a young person who has completed a course on anger management. They might use exercises that enable users to talk about their own experience and the distance they feel they have travelled. They may even be visual records, such as the photos of the graffiti before the 'clean up' of the estate and looking different afterwards.

- *Retrospective judgements about what people feel has improved*
  These are opinions gathered about what people feel when they look back. They are judgements about what feels different for them now compared with how they remember feeling before their contact with the service. They may be gathered through a structured format or through less formal qualitative interviews or exercises.

Most methods for evaluating outcomes adopt one or other of these approaches. They can be used with quantitative or qualitative data and they can deal with hard or soft outcomes and distance travelled. They may be used in more sophisticated 'randomised control trials' or 'quasi-experimental designs' to compare the change for the group that received the intervention against a control group that did not. In project evaluations where the resources are not available for large-scale studies, they are more usually used to document the changes that occurred in the group that used the service without the use of a control group.

Any of the data-collection methods may be appropriate. The questions centre on what your outcome target is, what difference you are seeking to demonstrate, what the indicators of change might be, what data is already available, how feasible it is to collect and analyse more, and what methods of information gathering may be most appropriate in your situation.

Methods of collecting the information

We know from our earlier discussion of indicators that for every indicator or measure you choose, there is almost always a decision to be made about *what* evidence you will collect for it and *how* you will collect that data. If one indicator is the opinions of elderly folk about their sense of safety on their local estate, those views could be collected through a postal survey or they could be gathered by local workers or interviewers in face-to-face conversations. Bell (1987) provides a useful account of how to select your methods of data collection (pp.53–100). There is also an overview of sources and methods in the online resources from the University of Wisconsin, where there are available more detailed downloads on several of the different methods (Taylor-Powell *et al.* 1996). The Charities Evaluation Service also offers examples of methods and data-collection tools (Ellis 2005). There are numerous other sources of help on the selection of methods in textbooks and online sources and we have listed some in Appendix B. Nearly all methods can provide both quantitative and qualitative data depending on how they are used but most tend more to one or the other and each has its own logistical problems. Table 7.1 sets out some of the main advantages and disadvantages of typical research methods that you might use for evaluation purposes and this may help you with the choices you need to make.

TABLE 7.1: A SUMMARY OF ADVANTAGES AND DISADVANTAGES
OF DIFFERENT EVALUATION METHODS

Evaluation method	Advantages	Disadvantages
Written questionnaire (with **closed** questions)	Can collect information quickly from a large sample Anonymity may encourage open response Can be simple to analyse	Survey overload can alienate people Difficult to ask the right questions clearly Response rate usually low Fears about literacy or limited English are a barrier
Written questionnaire (with **open** questions)	Allows people to express themselves more freely Richer responses than for closed questions Can be used in combination with structured questions	Free text responses are difficult and time consuming to analyse Some people cannot express themselves well in writing Response rate often low

It is also possible to mix both 'open' and 'closed' questions in a questionnaire (see 'Basic survey-design issues' p.145).

Online surveys	Can reach a wide audience relatively cheaply Can be structured to provide fast and automatic analysis of structured questions	Many clients in need do not have online access or do not have the skills or confidence to respond in this way Care is needed to ensure security of the site and protection of the identity of children or vulnerable adults Similar considerations apply as for written surveys
Individual interviews (face to face or by phone)	Interviewer can follow up answers and gain more detail Effective for collecting qualitative information Interviewee does not have to be able to read or write Generates a greater depth of response than other methods, especially if interviewer establishes good rapport Samples can be smaller but still yield high-quality data Can provide direct quotations	Takes considerable time, including setting up Respondents may miss interview or not respond well It needs well-prepared interviewers Needs schedule or topic guide Taping and transcription are costly. If they are not used, a data capture sheet or recording system is needed for notes People may feel awkward if interviewed by someone who knows them More time and skill needed to analyse responses
Group interviews or focus groups	Can gather views from a larger number of people Can explore opinions of a group rather than just those of individuals Less time consuming than one to one Relatively inexpensive Can provide quotes from the discussion	Requires setting up time and a topic guide or plan Needs skill to keep the discussion moving and to the point Not helpful for sensitive or confidential issues Difficult to take notes of a fast-moving discussion. A note-taker or tape recorder can be helpful but tapes will then need transcribing Qualitative responses may be hard to analyse Dominant group members or peer pressure may bias responses

TABLE 7.1 (CONTINUED)

Evaluation method	Advantages	Disadvantages
Document analysis	Can be used to analyse case records, or other written or published material Can be useful for collecting baseline data Capitalises on existing information Requires description of how the sample of documents was taken	Needs to be systematic to be valid Requires a consistent system or coding for content analysis Can be time consuming Data may have been collected for another purpose and may be inadequate in format or detail
Case studies	Provides an in-depth picture of one case with the client's needs and progress in context Can include quotations from clients themselves and other players	Ideally requires several sources of information to provide a complete picture and triangulation Can be an over-used method Superficial case studies do not impress. Need to show clear outcomes Single cases need to be backed up by wider data
Diaries and logs	May be able to capture critical incidents as part of progress record Provides a chronological record	Need to be well structured and regularly completed Qualitative material may be complex to analyse
Observation	Can capture behaviour without disrupting activity Can assess the delivery of the programme as it happens and capture the dynamics of the situation	Needs an observation checklist and skill in what to look for Requires trained observers May be difficult to analyse results Observation or filming can influence the behaviour of the individuals involved
Reflection and feedback exercises	Numerous variations available Can use visual material Stimulates response and helps to capture soft outcomes Can help client identify and value their own progress Can easily be integrated in everyday practice Can be fun	Must be used consistently to be useful for evaluation Needs recording immediately before context of response is lost May be hard to understand what people's comments mean

Tests and assessments	Can produce quantitative measures or scores Can test factual knowledge and certain skills with reasonable ease and accuracy Can be used in an informal/fun way such as quizzes or card tests	May be forbidding for participants, especially where education has been a barrier Can be stressful – many people fear giving a 'wrong answer' or being marked Psychological tests need expertise: should be used with proper safeguards
Drawings	Can be used effectively with children or people with certain difficulties in communication or understanding Can provide vivid illustrations for a report Good for a 'before and after' description	Drawings need a commentary or labels to explain to the reader what they meant to the client 'Draw and write' may work better where appropriate Reproduction of the drawing in a report may be technically difficult and will require permission

All the above methods may need adjustment for respondents with physical disabilities or learning difficulties or certain health conditions. Even then, in some cases, the method will not be suitable.

Ethical principles such as confidentiality or gaining properly informed consent should be applied in all these methods. Almost all research methods may in some way raise emotional or disturbing issues for respondents and appropriate safeguards must therefore be considered (see Chapter 5 'Protecting children and vulnerable adults').

Practice example

VCS Matters is a partnership-led third sector programme set up in spring 2007 with BVSC – the Centre for Voluntary Action (Birmingham Voluntary Service Council) as the accountable body. It facilitates the appropriate engagement of the third sector in the *Every Child Matters* agenda and local Children's Trust arrangements. It was originally funded by the Children's Fund and, more recently, by the local authority to help ensure that the voluntary sector was properly consulted and involved in the development of children's services. With a small staff and wide-ranging outcomes, it has been faced with a challenge in covering such a daunting remit and showing evidence of its impact in a limited time.

In October 2007, VCS Matters had to report on progress for the funding review for the following financial year. An e-mail survey was sent to contacts on the mailing list, asking how satisfied they were with the progress of VCS Matters, whether or not it had improved their knowledge of current developments in services for children and young people and whether it had increased their understanding of the need for engagement with the Children's Trust arrangements. Each question was answered on a scale of 1 to 5 (1 not at all; 2 not really; 3 a little; 4 quite a lot; 5 very much). Respondents could also offer their own comments.

This yielded good scores including for the outcome-orientated questions on increased knowledge of developments and understanding of the Trust arrangements. The qualitative comments were reported in full and the majority were very positive including: 'an excellent and informative website'; 'increased knowledge of the commissioning process and how to get the best out of it'; 'a bigger and more coordinated voice for VCS'; 'our meetings have given me insights as well as contacts with the key partners'.

The programme also undertook a baseline survey in summer 2007, repeated in autumn 2008 so that it could compare opinions over time. Comparison of these surveys showed minor gains in scores on how respondents perceived their knowledge about several specific Children's Trust developments and more substantial gains on scores about how much influence the voluntary and community sector was seen as having in Trust arrangements.

This work illustrates how an infrastructure programme that does not directly serve clients in the community still has to evidence its outcomes. It also shows the use of an e-mail survey, comparison of scaled scores against a baseline and the effective use of some quantitative measures mixed with qualitative comment.

Peer evaluation

Most of the methods above could be used in what is known as 'peer evaluation'. This approach involves service users or their peers (people of the same age group or sharing the same characteristics as the beneficiaries of the service under evaluation). It has considerable attractions and funders often warm to it because it offers a clear user perspective.

The advantages of involving peer researchers include:

- the opportunity to draw on the insights of people who either are clients of the service or share their circumstances in some way. Evaluators cannot often offer those perspectives from their own experience (for example, what it is like to be an adolescent at the present time, or what it feels like to be on the receiving end of attitudes towards people with disabilities)

- easier access to the views of the group in question. Clients, for instance, who feel the interviewer shares some of their experience may open up more easily. Where groups are hard to contact, peer researchers who understand the context may help to build up a good sample

- the spin-offs in the lives of the peer evaluators themselves may be substantial. They will feel respected and trusted and may gain payment or qualifications or be able to add the experience to their CVs.

There are, however, many considerations if this approach is to be adopted because it has both difficulties and risks involved. These include:

- the need to train the peer evaluators properly. This will involve both an explanation of the methods to be used and an understanding of the ethical issues entailed (such as confidentiality)

- even so, peer evaluators may not produce records or interview notes of the highest quality as their skills will often be as yet undeveloped. This may involve the lead evaluator in more work at the writing-up stage

- selection can present difficulties. A peer research group needs to include a diversity of individuals, not simply the hand-picked few who are already enthusiastic about the programme

- peer evaluators should be properly recognised. They should not be exploited. This will involve at least the payment of expenses but will usually involve a fee or part-time salary

- such projects need to be properly resourced. There will be training costs in some form for the peer evaluators and other resources may be required, such as travel expenses or access to computers

- accreditation of their learning and contribution is one of the best means of showing proper recognition. This can take significant time and effort to set up and in some cases, such as accreditation that requires production of a portfolio, can involve the peer evaluator in considerable extra work

- it is important to understand the demands and pressures on the lives of peer evaluators. They will have school, study, work, family and friends to cope with as well as the project and may have other needs arising from complexities in their own experience such as health needs or cultural issues. It has also been found in particular that young people who become involved in such participative projects tend to receive disproportionate requests to contribute to other initiatives as well. (Skinner and Fleming 2007; Sloan 2007)

Practice example

Project Re:action was a Big Lottery funded joint research project between Youth Action Network, a national volunteering charity and the Centre for Social Action at De Montfort University. It aimed to find out more about the experience of young people who volunteer and its outcomes, and the difference that full participation makes to the volunteering experience.

In keeping with the ethos of the project, young people themselves were fully involved in planning, steering and carrying out the research. Training and accreditation were provided for 35 young volunteers who acted as peer researchers and/or members of a steering group. They helped develop the methodology and carried out qualitative focus groups with young people. They were provided with a laptop and, where possible, subsidised internet connection so that they could make records and communicate easily with other project members.

The findings show significant outcomes from a well-supported volunteering experience, especially the increase in social capital for the young people involved. 'Social capital' means the resource that stems from people's social interactions and network opportunities, which take place in specific environments. In this case the context was the volunteering experience and young people developed their social networks with benefits, from personal and emotional support to more career opportunities. In some settings there were gains in social cohesion in their local communities. 'Community cohesion' is about bridging gaps, changing or challenging structures or interacting with people of other communities. Over 60 per cent of the young people surveyed perceived their volunteering as bringing different people from their community or neighbourhood together or helping others to be more active in their own locality. The research found that where young people experience high levels of trust from adults and full participation, they tend to make bigger gains in their own lives. Where they feel they are trusted to take on responsibility there is less likelihood of negative outcomes from the volunteering experience, such as stress or disillusionment.

Seven of the young people themselves were interviewed by a visiting researcher in an evaluation of the project's work in promoting participation in the research. Their comments give a feel of what the project meant to them.

I liked the look of it [Project Re:action] – *it was actually trying to find something out. And we weren't just being asked questions, it was like 'get your hands in there' and looking at it and learning about it – learning different skills. And the fact that it was all youth-led was really attractive. Often these projects are just adults saying 'OK, do this, do that'.* (p.11.)

For me personally, I didn't know I'd be able to do these things, as a young person – for example, data analysis. I didn't know we'd be sitting in a room looking at questions that young people have answered and analysing it. We thought, oh we'll just do the focus groups and run the sessions, but the adults will do it [the analysis] *after. So that's been a big step I think.* (p.13)

(Boeck 2009)

Samples

Whatever methods you are choosing to use to evaluate, the question will arise of how you selected individual respondents or documentary evidence. If time, resource constraints or other practical difficulties mean that you cannot include all your potential respondents or sources in your evaluation a sample may be necessary. As stressed in Chapter 6, the way in which you choose your sample and how representative it is will affect the credibility of your findings. Denscombe and Ellis both offer helpful basic accounts of how to choose your sample, the main types of samples and how to avoid bias in your selection (Denscombe 2005, pp.12–27; Ellis 2005, pp.105–107).

In order to take a sample you first have to define the 'population' from which you wish to draw the sample. For instance, a population might be every homeless person who stayed in an agency's hostel provision for any length of time during a particular period. To take a random sample of this group you need to be sure that you can identify who is in this population or be aware of where a complete list exists already.

The gold standard of sampling is the 'probability' or 'random sample'; this is where every person in the population under study has an equal chance of being selected, rather like an unbiased lottery draw where every number has an equal chance of being drawn. The system is completely random (so that it is impossible to predict what number will come up). If you have a complete list (numbered for each case), selection can be made using random number tables (available free on the Internet and in statistical texts). A total sample (taking everybody in the group under study) is also a random sample because everybody is automatically selected without bias.

You could also take a 'systematic sample' by starting at a random point found by throwing a dice or similar and taking, say, every tenth name. For example, a specialist social-work intervention may only have been offered to 40 clients during the year. A sample of 10 might be randomly selected for an in-depth evaluation interview by starting at a random point and taking every fourth name.

A 'stratified random sample' is one where the population is subdivided into its important constituent groups and the random sample is drawn within those groups. For example, you might have relatively few female users but need to be sure that both men and women are included in a survey. In a simple random sample, the women could be missed by chance. In this situation you could divide your list of users into male and female and sample randomly within both groups, but you should be careful not to impose too many of your own theories about which differences in your population are most important.

If such random samples are large enough, the views of the respondents or facts about them can be seen as being representative of the whole group. Given the total number in the sample and the statistical tests applied, mathematical rules enable statistical findings to be stated with a certain 'level of confidence'. This means that at a certain level we can be confident that the probability of the effects observed being mistaken or simply down to chance is extremely small and that the results are 'statistically significant'. Although it probably goes against our instincts, it is the absolute number in the sample not the proportion of the whole 'population' in question that affects this confidence about how representative the sample is. The larger the number in your sample, the more confidence can be attached to it and where your total numbers are small anyway (say fewer than 100) you would be well advised to try to get a 100 per cent sample if you can. In many evaluations reporting statistical results you will see a value for 'p' or 'probability'. For example, a level of confidence of 0.05 means that we can be 95 per cent confident that the results are not just due to chance or error. So any test result which has a 'p' or probability value of less than 0.05 can be considered significant at this level of confidence. If you need to show statistically significant results in this way, to demonstrate with confidence that particular outcomes are linked to a specific intervention, it would be wise to involve a statistician unless this is within your own field of expertise.

Practice example

In order to evaluate the effect of the 'Crash Course' road-safety education scheme provided by Staffordshire Fire and Rescue Service and its partners, evaluators carried out a large-scale survey of pupils in the participating secondary schools. The course covers nearly all schools in the county.

To ensure a sufficiently large return and a representative sample, all the schools, colleges and training providers taking bookings for the autumn term 2008 were asked to administer 'before' and 'after' questionnaires. All institutions booking the Crash Course in the spring term 2009 were similarly asked to administer the questions to the 'control group'. Since this gave near universal coverage of the organisations educating young people in the relevant age group, no sampling was undertaken (though the schools and colleges were later coded for an estimate of local deprivation levels to enable an analysis of whether deprivation affected the results).

Returns were received from schools, etc. that received Crash Course in the autumn term and from those that would have the presentation in the spring. Diligent follow-up was required in order to minimise the level of non-response. A total of 1,717 valid questionnaires were returned, with some 998 from schools that had received the course and 719 from those that had not. It was also possible to match some 290 young people for their 'before' and 'after' responses.

This enabled the evaluators to provide valid statistical results and state clearly the level of confidence that could be attached to them. Several statistical tests were used including the Mann Whitney test which examines the degree of difference between two groups and, for the 'before' and 'after' situation, the Wilcoxon test which tests the differences between matched pairs. The evidence showed that the course did have a positive impact on attitudes to road safety amongst the pupils who had received it. For instance, it had a consistently positive effect on attitudes towards the wearing of seat-belts. At a statistically significant level, of those who completed the matched 'before' and 'after' questionnaires, more young people felt it was acceptable always to wear a seat-belt after the course than before (Wilcoxon test, $p<0.001$). Comparing those who attended the course with those who had not, the effect was similar (Mann Whitney test, $p=0.034$). The comparison between those who *had* experienced the course and those who *had not* shows statistically significant higher total scores on the questions designed to test knowledge of the key causes of road collisions (Mann Whitney test, p=0.001). The qualitative evidence confirmed the positive effects shown in the survey.

(Hoggarth *et al.* 2009a, unpublished)

If your list is not up to date, or is incomplete in other ways, then you have an inadequate sampling frame. For example, you might not have a complete register of project participants or be able to produce a comprehensive list of all your stakeholders. In many situations the size of the population under study (e.g. beneficiaries in the community or people who are using illegal drugs) is just not known: no complete list exists or some clients are unavailable or difficult to contact.

For these reasons in many community projects – and a great deal of other research – 'non-probability sampling' is undertaken. This refers to the many ways of selecting a sample that are alternatives to taking a random sample. Each method has value as well as limitations:

- You might, for instance, take what is called a 'purposive sample', which means you deliberately select a number of people who meet each criterion you want such as being of a particular age group or ethnicity or having undertaken the same activity. This gives you a cross-section of your users.

- You could also use a 'snowballing sample', especially where the group may be resistant to outsiders or hard to contact. Here the first few people you talk to are asked to suggest, say, two other people who share the characteristics you are looking for and so on, until you have a large enough sample.

If you want to show correlations (the links between two factors, for example, undertaking a particular course and then obtaining employment) or other forms of valid statistics then you will need a randomly selected sample of sufficient size. The necessary size of sample is determined by statistical rules that take into account the types of test to be applied and the number of variables under consideration, and so it is prudent to take expert advice if statistical validity is needed. Even where you are not intending to use statistical measures, you may want to use tables or categories to analyse your results by sub-sets and you will need a sample that provides meaningful numbers (say five or more) in each category. A table that compares, for example, three grades of achievement for boys against girls will have six possible categories. If only small numbers were used it would not only be statistically invalid but would look ridiculous as there would only be one or two in each 'box' of the table.

Whatever type of sample you choose in the end, you should give a clear account of how it was determined. The reader should be able to understand how many respondents were selected, the size of the total list (or 'population'), the tests or comparisons you applied and the level of validity you are claiming.

Basic survey-design issues

Where written surveys are used, the commonest pitfall after those associated with sampling is the issue of the clarity of the questions. To some extent the same problems apply to surveys administered face to face or to interview questions but where the interviewer is present, it is easier to clarify a particular question.

Survey design is a skill in its own right. There are online survey programmes available for a fee, which will usually also offer a facility for analysis of the results. Use of such systems can be worthwhile but the disadvantage is that it is more difficult to tailor the questions precisely for your own situation, and some can only be answered on line. An Internet search on 'questionnaire design' will offer you such commercial templates and plenty of information on how to design your questions (e.g. Creative Research Systems 2009; University of Leeds 2009). There is also helpful material in books on research methods (e.g. Bell 1987; Foddy 1993; Munn and Drewer 2004).

If you are designing your own questionnaire, spend time reflecting on what the essential questions are that will produce evidence that relates to your outcomes. Space is at a premium in surveys and you should not waste it on questions that may be interesting but do not yield the evidence you need. Keep it simple: drop the questions that would be just 'nice to know'. You will also need questions that obtain sufficient detail for your purposes about the respondent.

Choosing the form of the questions

In terms of the format of the questions, the first decision is whether you want to have 'closed questions' (which produce easily quantifiable answers), or 'open questions' (to obtain more descriptive qualitative answers). It is also possible to have a mixture of both.

'Open questions' ask for an answer in the respondent's own words, whether as a word, a phrase or an extended comment. For example, you might ask 'Can you give us an example of something that has improved for you as a result of taking part in this project? If so, please describe how things have changed in the box below?'

'Closed questions' are structured questions that force the respondent to choose a response (or responses) from amongst a given set of options.

Closed questions come in many different forms. The choices can be given, for example, as:

- a list of possible answers (such as 'yes', 'no' or 'don't know')
- a set of categories
- a choice of rank order (where number 1 usually indicates the highest priority)
- scales (such as five points on a continuum from 'strongly agree' to 'strongly disagree')
- grids
- quantities (where the options are in numbers such as 'How many job applications have you made in the past year? Please tick.').

Wording your questions

Some further general guidance on formulating questions is now summarised below:

- Try to start with the easy questions that are relevant to the people in your sample. Progress to the more sensitive or difficult ones later. Consider leaving personal demographic details, like questions about age, gender or ethnic group, to the end.
- You should make clear how precisely the question should be answered. For example, you should state whether the respondent is only allowed to choose one option out of a list or as many as they wish (as in '*tick all that apply to you*').
- Categories should be clear and not overlapping so that the respondent can only fit one category. If age categories are offered, you should use for instance 0–9, 10–19, 20–29 and not 0–10, 10–20, 20–30.
- Avoid ambiguous, imprecise or 'double-barrelled' questions. For example, it is impossible to answer the following questions because their meaning is not clear.
  - *'Have you felt that your health or family relationships have improved? Yes/No.'*
    (Here two options are wrapped up in the same question. The respondent may feel that family relationships are better but not their health.)

- ○ *'How often have you attended the project recently?'*
  (To answer the question, the respondent needs to know what 'recently' means: is it the last week or the last six months?)

- Make sure any options you give are as complete as possible but don't force the choices on the person answering. You will still need to include categories for 'other', or 'not applicable' or 'don't know' to be sure every respondent can give a logical and honest answer. If it is a very personal question, you might include a 'decline to respond' option.

- Avoid leading questions (ones that presume a certain answer). These include examples such as

  - ○ *'Please detail the benefits you have experienced from the counselling?'*
    (This assumes that the respondent has benefited and does not allow them the option to say they have not) or

  - ○ *'Do you not agree that the treatment has improved your condition?'*
    (This puts pressure on the respondent to answer in a particular way).

- Try to use a simple horizontal or vertical format on your questionnaire form. Grids or several columns of answer choices are difficult for most people to understand and fill in.

- Try to avoid too many contingency questions. This means questions that subdivide into further questions like *'Did you lose weight?' Yes/No.* 'If Yes, how much weight did you lose? If No, go to Question 8'.

- Avoid negative questions such as *'Do you think you have not learned anything on this course?'* Most people will misunderstand and treat these as positive questions.

- Leave enough space for people to write if you use open questions. Four or five lines is a good guideline.

- Avoid asking questions that people in your sample will not have the knowledge to answer or where they may not understand the terms you use.

- Be aware of cultural factors such as sensitive issues around terms referring to religious faith or family structures, or the tendency in some cultures to exaggerate answers or conform to perceived expectations.

- Avoid discriminatory language. Use terms that show respect to your respondent.

Layout

Once you have designed your questions, you need to consider the layout of your questionnaire with a view to getting the best possible response. Your questionnaire should be given a title, a date and a friendly introduction that explains its purpose clearly and identifies the sponsoring agency. It should also be made to look as attractive as possible, perhaps with a logo, picture or some colour in the text. Children respond well to pictures and symbols. Try to avoid a crowded look with too many questions to a page (and remember that very small print can put people off or exclude people with visual impairment). Instructions should be clear about how questions should be answered, the closing date and where to send or hand in the completed questionnaire. These instructions should be printed on the questionnaire itself in case it is separated from other papers, and a stamped addressed envelope should be supplied if appropriate. Some form of thanks for completion should also be included. Above all, the questionnaire should not be too long: most people get weary or careless when faced with numerous pages to fill in and some will not even attempt it.

The need for a pilot

Perhaps the most important piece of advice we can give you is to pilot your questionnaire. This means testing it out on a small number of people who are typical of your sample. You need to check:

- if the questions are understood
- if any of the format confuses people, leaves their answers uncertain or puts them off, and
- whether you can analyse the responses to produce the sort of evidence you need.

Make absolutely sure that the details of how to return the response are clear and that they will work in your situation.

Setting up data-collection systems

All projects need some form of record-keeping. Most will have written case files or computer-based records on individuals in spreadsheet or database format. This can be a rich source of evaluation information and, moreover, you can ensure you get 'two for the price of one' if you set up your record-keeping to provide some outcome data as well as the basic details of clients and interventions or activities.

Whether you intend to keep written records or computerised data, it is possible to incorporate the question of outcomes into your recording system. To be of maximum use, this information needs to relate directly to the outcomes set for the particular service or project. Manual case files are easy to access and usually allow staff a certain amount of freedom in the way they are completed. Computerised records are less flexible but deal with large amounts of information more efficiently. Database systems will have a unique reference number or identifier for each individual client and can therefore be used to provide information on the relationship between factors. For example, you might wish to know whether minority ethnic participants achieved the same level of outcomes as white participants. A database can be programmed to provide that information, whereas it would have to be separately extracted from individual case files.

In setting up such systems it is important to watch out for typical pitfalls:

- It is crucial to reflect on what evidence you need *before* setting up your system. It is almost always impossible to go back and add more fields or questions for completion later. In any case, adding questions later will usually mean that you cannot include cases completed before that in any total sample

- Pilot the system to make sure it is easily understood and workable. Test computer programmes to make sure they will produce the information in the form you need it.

- Take advice before setting up computerised records, particularly database systems, unless you are an expert yourself. Considerable money and energy is spent on computer systems that do not yield the supposed results and most projects can ill afford such mistakes.

- Once the format for the case files or database is established, staff will need to be familiarised with what is required. It is essential that workers grasp the need to complete all fields properly or you may end up with large sections of missing data.

- Make sure that more than one person in the organisation knows how to enter and extract information from any computerised system in case of absence or illness.

- Data input and completion of records should take place regularly before people's memories fade or information is lost. Beware of allowing backlogs of data input to mount up.

- The collection of data on individuals on computer may require registration under the Data Protection Act 1998 (see Chapter 5). Information from such registered files should not be disclosed to outside enquirers except under clear inter-agency protocols in the circumstances allowed by law, such as protecting children or preventing crime.

Activity

Reflect on the data your project or service collects as part of its everyday routine.

- What information currently exists about your service users in files or on computer in your agency?

- Does this give you any help on evaluation issues?

- Does it include information relating to the outcomes for participants?

- If not, how could it be structured to increase its usefulness for outcome evaluation?

- Are there any new projects where a clean start could be made on what data should be collected?

- How could it be made most useful, not only for collecting outputs but also for showing outcomes?

Choosing the 'best fit' methods

There is no magic answer to the question of how to choose the best methods for your purpose. Your approach has to fit the context of your own service. There are some key issues that may, however, help your considerations.

- The methods chosen should be applied in order to provide you with evidence about outcomes. The most sophisticated evaluation designs may still not produce such evidence unless the questions asked deal with the changes or benefits resulting from the scheme.

- Methods for seeking the views of your respondents should be tailored to their abilities and social and cultural background. Younger children or people with learning difficulties, for example, will not cope with long written questionnaires – they may need simple questions, perhaps with symbols or illustrations, or a method that does not require writing at all. At the other end of the spectrum, stakeholders in senior roles may not be able to offer an hour or more for an intensive interview.

- The method should be appropriate for gathering the sort of information you require. If you want the words of the participants themselves or the detail of their perceptions then 'closed' questions are not suitable. If you need large numbers of responses analysed quickly, then 'closed' questions may be exactly what you need.

- A balance of quantitative and qualitative methods is usually desirable.

- The methods chosen need to win over the respondent and make them want to express their views. Evaluation exercises can be presented in a fun way; questions can be framed in simple, down-to-earth language; interviews can convey a real interest in those responding and a realistic chance of improving services.

- The methods you choose need to be practical and achievable within the time and resources you have available. It is better to produce *some* evidence however small within your own competence and capacity than to be over-ambitious and end up with nothing useful to say about the outcomes of your project.

- You should only make proportionate demands of the service and those who are asked to respond. To give an obvious example, it is not reasonable to expect a patient who is in pain to talk to an evaluator for an hour and a half of intensive questioning. Nor is it realistic to undertake a survey of 1,000 people for a project receiving £10,000 in funding.

- The methods need to be appropriate for the intended readership and the expectations of the audience. If large-scale statistical measures are expected, it is tempting providence to submit a CD of video evidence.

- The methods must be ethical in principle and practical safeguards must be in place. If it is not possible to gain parental consent, for instance, to interview young children, then it is wisest not to include this approach in the design.

Practice example

Numerous claims are made for the benefits of sport, including informal sports activities. These include such outcomes as engaging young people who 'slip through the net', reducing community tensions and youth crime, and promoting health through moderate exercise or reduced misuse of drugs (Office of the Deputy Prime Minister 2004). Sports organisations are waking up to the necessity of evidencing outcomes but this is not always easy in practice. Methods need to be suitable for young people immersed in an activity they enjoy and need to show qualitative as well as quantitative evidence of change.

Kickz – Goals through Football is an organisation supported by the Football Foundation and the police. It uses the power of football and the appeal of professional clubs to target 12–18 year olds in some highly disadvantaged areas, offering activities three nights a week on 48 weeks of the year. It aims to reduce crime and anti-social behaviour; increase playing, coaching and officiating opportunities for participants; increase volunteering; and help create routes into education, training and employment.

To facilitate the monitoring and evaluation of Kickz, their evaluators provide all projects with a web-based system that provides a number of tools to collect and report on project progress. The uniform system across all the projects means that data can be aggregated over the whole programme. This includes key statistics on the demographic details of participants, attendance and engagement in skill development, and volunteering. It also collects qualitative evidence including photographs, video clips and evidence of young people's work. Other partner data is also collected especially on crime and anti-social behaviour.

This enables Kickz to show, for instance, the profile of participants, the numbers attending and the geographical areas served. Links can clearly be made between the activities and the outcomes in *Every Child Matters* and the targets of local authorities. Outcomes can be evidenced in the qualifications and accreditation gained by the participants and volunteer roles taken up. Reductions in local crime figures for those offences most associated with young people and the incidence of anti-social behaviour can be shown in many areas where the scheme operates by comparing data year-on-year or comparing times when the scheme is operating with days when it is not. This is not conclusive evidence of the football activities as a causal factor but it evidences a potential contribution. The figures are backed up by numerous case studies, photographs and comments from partners. The 2008 report covers the first two years of the scheme. It makes compelling reading. Good evaluation systems and the use of varied methods have enabled the organisation to provide a comprehensive portrait of its work.

(Football Foundation and Substance 2008)

Keeping it practical

Above all it is essential that your methods for collecting evaluation information are practical and realistic. As we explained in the discussion of planning and logistics in Chapter 4, the time, resources, levels of skills and access to data we have at our disposal should all be key factors in our decisions about evaluation methods. Too many evaluators pick their methods without reflection on what is involved in seeing them through.

Timing is of the essence: this is the factor in our experience where a large proportion of evaluation effort runs aground. Workers simply underestimate how long it takes to set things up, or fail to allow sufficient time for data analysis and writing up. Certain methods can also turn out to be impractical because they are too costly to implement and the use of existing data may be more cost effective than gathering new information. Other methods may not be feasible because access to the information may not be granted or the respondents may be too difficult to contact or unwilling to take part. If an organisation is in turmoil due to being in the throes of a reorganisation, staff morale is likely to be low and it may not be realistic to expect all staff to return a written questionnaire or afford time for an interview.

The skills of those who will implement the methods are also critical. As a case in point, it requires real skills to get the best from an interview, drawing out the perceptions of the interviewee and capturing their comments in comprehensive notes or tapes for transcription. Trying to elicit findings from badly conducted interviews is soul-destroying work, so training and practice may be necessary to get the best out of this method of data-gathering.

Now you have given some more thought to your methods and their advantages and disadvantages, you may well wish to revisit your work plan to check its feasibility. Remember, it needs to be reasonable, practical and 'do-able'!

CHAPTER 8

Evaluation Tools and How to Use Them Effectively

In Chapter 7, we gave you a snapshot of the wealth of data you could choose to collect in order to show evidence of the benefits to your service users. We also weighed up some of the advantages and disadvantages of different data-collection methods and offered practical guidance on designing questions and record systems. Usually you will be seeking to show outcomes by measuring your indicators against a baseline, measuring changes over the period of intervention or gathering retrospective views about what people feel has changed for the better. And, as discussed, whichever approach you use, the issue of ethics will come into play as the safeguarding of your participants is always your first priority. In this chapter, we offer some advice about the implementation of your choice of method especially using the tools that can show up soft outcomes. All the methods we have discussed so far can be used to demonstrate change, whether it is in 'hard' outcome measures or in distance travelled. It is, however, important to implement them properly and consistently to get the best results, and this chapter explores what that means in practice.

Existing surveys and assessment systems

Online survey systems and resources for assessment have become much more widely available in recent years, partly because of the demand for outcome evidence. Many of these systems are available commercially, and training is often available on their use. One of the best-known examples is the Framework for the Assessment of Children in Need and their Families, which is published jointly by several government departments (Department of Health, Department for Education and Employment and Home Office 2000). This offers a framework, practice guidance and a range of questionnaires on the website such as the Family Pack of Questionnaires and Scales, Parenting Daily Hassles, Adult Wellbeing, or Adolescent Wellbeing. Outcomes can be assessed as movement in scores on the scaled questions. The Strengths and Difficulties questionnaire in the series is still being used with children in some local authorities to assess their progress towards the outcomes of *Every Child Matters*.

Many other systems are commercially available, such as the Rickter Scale – which is particularly suitable for use with young people and has been used in national provision such as the Connexions Service. This asks the client to assess themselves on a board device with a physical sliding scale on which they can move a pointer to indicate their view of their own position against selected indicators such as family relationships or the suitability of their accommodation. Numerous sets of indicators are available to choose from. There are paper-based aids to evaluation and assessment such as those promoted by Alcohol Concern, the Soul Record, Evaluation Support Scotland or the National Youth Agency: some of which have built-in scoring systems. There are also many media-based approaches on sale including software packages for cartooning (useful for getting participants to produce a cartoon of their own progress), touch-screen responses or recording of video evidence. Online entries can change very quickly but if you search the Internet on topics like 'evaluation tools' or 'evaluation design' or 'evaluation' with particular groups such as 'young people', you will find plenty of leads on what is currently available.

Clearly, you will need to reflect carefully before buying into a pre-designed system so as to make sure it will fit the needs of your agency and be able to give evidence of your outcomes. It's also important to be aware that some of these questionnaires and assessment systems have been rigorously tested and have a high degree of reliability – meaning that the research tool works consistently and the variations in results can be put down to differences amongst those responding rather than to variations in how the research tool itself is working. If you choose to use a questionnaire or scale like this it is therefore important not to modify it; it is also vital to process the responses exactly as specified in the authentic implementation guide. However tempting it is to adapt and customise, you will only obtain valid results if you use the tool as it is designed.

Using your own questionnaires and interview schedules

If you design your own surveys or interview schedules, the guidance in Chapter 7 on framing questions applies and the need to be rigorous in their use becomes even more important. It is critical to pilot your initial design to be sure that your questions are clear and that they yield the information you need in a form that can be analysed fairly easily. Make sure that those who are distributing questionnaires (such as project staff or teachers in a school setting) understand how to introduce them properly. Set up a filing system early on, with a reference number for each questionnaire return or set of interview notes – do not be tempted to leave piles of unsorted responses for later.

People often think that interviewing is easy and anybody could do it. In fact, interviewers need some skill and practice and even for the most experienced a new schedule of questions should be tried out first. It is worth getting someone to practise the introduction and the process of asking for consent as well as the questions. Interviews can be highly structured, giving people limited choices in their answers or they may be semi-structured with some open questions and the interviewer will often be asked to follow up points of interest as they emerge. It is useful to write some prompts and points to probe on the schedule as it is often such follow-up questions that yield the most telling information.

You should be clear in instructions to interviewers if any questions are absolutely necessary and must be covered. A standard recording sheet on which the interviewer can note the main points is often helpful. This may be just a sheet with the questions and space to write notes on the answers or it may give the interviewer a format such as options to tick depending on the responses. Interviews can be taped but material gathered will then need transcribing and sifting and that can be expensive and time consuming. Also, some people find tape recording intimidating and for some it is an unpleasant reminder of police station interviews. If you have to write up interviews or transcribe tapes, then do so as soon as you possibly can. Queries become much harder to sort out as memory fades, which means that valuable evidence can be lost or simply never used.

Sometimes you may need to code information, especially if you have a large number of interviews or questionnaires. That means giving a number or 'code' to a category of response so that the results can be entered on a spreadsheet or database. This may be a code for basic characteristics or responses (such as $1 = $ Yes, $2 = $ No and $3 = $ Don't Know). It can also be a set of codes for themes that you are identifying for your context from the material, such as health problems mentioned or difficulties experienced in parenting. Think out your coding list as early as possible and start entering up the coded data regularly as you go along. That process can show up additional categories you need and will help you to avoid a backlog at the analysis stage.

The issue of sampling was explored in the last chapter. It is important for your design to decide the number of responses you need and how the respondents will be selected but this needs continued attention in the implementation stages too. You will always need to follow up in order to minimise non-response. When you are gathering responses through surveys or interviews, it is also important to record the number and the characteristics of those who respond as a proportion of all those who could be involved, as you will need this in your presentation of results. Make a careful note of who does not respond and (if possible) state why, as this can also affect the credibility of your sample.

Project records as a source of evidence

Most projects will be keeping some form of records of progress for their users, whether as case files or databases. These can be used to capture both hard and soft outcomes.

A database can be used to generate considerable amounts of information because it can relate each participant to the interventions received, activities undertaken and the outcomes achieved. A project dealing with offenders could for example use a database to record:

- a reference number for the individual

- the contact details

- the reason for referral

- the position at different stages on some form of assessment

- activities undertaken

- outcomes such as whether or not there were further offences, whether new educational qualifications were achieved, or entry into training or employment.

If presented anonymously, this information can provide collated results suitable for use in evaluation, such as how many of the group had offended again or had reported gains in improved relationships with their families.

Case files will need more reading time and they may need coding for analysis of certain themes or factors (see Chapter 9, 'Interpreting survey data'). They can usefully provide a wealth of information such as client details, the length of time they have been in contact with the agency, the nature of the presenting problems, the types of support offered and evidence of progress made. Useful quotations from workers or clients might also have been recorded. If case files or databases can be set up so as to include the purpose of collecting outcome information, then the process of using them for evaluation will be much simpler. The cautions in using such sources are that the evaluator needs to be absolutely sure that:

- the permissions are in place to use the data for this purpose
- the guidance on sampling is applied so that cases are not 'cherry picked'
- that all personal identifying details are removed from reports.

Case studies

Case studies, on the other hand, are often specially selected – usually to show the work of an agency in a good light. For this reason they should be treated with caution and should never be used as the sole evidence for outcomes. Where they are used well, they do nevertheless, portray the detail of the user's situation in a way that facts and figures cannot do, and they illustrate more fully how the organisation has worked with the user to achieve progress. The material for a case study should be drawn if possible from different sources, so as to 'triangulate' the evidence. Case files, interviews with the user or the staff who worked with them, comments from other people who know the user, and evaluation comments from the individual themselves can all be used to build up the picture. It is important to convey some specific details on age, gender and social situation in order to give the reader some background. Case studies can show the situation 'before' and 'after' but in any case for this context, they must show evidence of positive outcomes. As our example of a case study illustrates, very often these underline the qualities of the relationship with the worker, frequently seen as 'someone who believes in me and is there for me', and the huge significance of that dynamic for people who have been dealt such poor cards.

Practice example

The Birmingham Resettlement Mentoring Forum was a 'Test Bed Initiative' funded by the West Midlands Learning and Skills Council and led by the New Hope Mentoring Programme. Its aim was to link together several local organisations offering mentoring so that any client leaving prison and needing mentoring could be appropriately placed with one of the signatory agencies. In 2008/9, an independent evaluation was commissioned from Wider Impact Consultancy to detail the partnership's work and assess the effectiveness of mentoring as an intervention. Several different approaches were adopted to help evidence the outcomes of the process, including a number of case studies – one of which is reproduced here with the permission of the client and the agency. Details given by the offender were checked by the evaluators with the mentoring agency and with the police to ensure accuracy. Pseudonyms were used to ensure anonymity. The case study was produced from interviews with the mentee at two stages of the intervention and is therefore able to describe the 'distance travelled' in the client's own words. It also illustrates the nature of the support provided in the mentoring relationship, how significant that is for the positive outcomes and the importance of offering it promptly at the tipping point when motivation to change is high.

Part 1 – May 2007

Claire is 22 years old… Her mentor is Sharon aged 29 years. Claire's life was OK until she left school at 15 to live with a 19-year-old boy. *'My mum was not happy about it, which looking back, helped me to justify what I did – I was rebelling.'*

It took Claire a while to realise he was taking hard drugs in front of her. *'I hadn't got a clue what he was doing when he smoked heroin in front of me. I just knew he was a nicer person when he did, so I joined in… I was so naïve. I suppose I became his drugs partner.*

I had a good job earning us £100 a week, but by the time I was 16, I was addicted to heroin and had to let the job go. Looking back I now realise how bad he was. He broke into my mum's house and I never believed it until now. I had to go shoplifting for money for the heroin and he used to hit me a lot. I ended up in prison by the time I was 17, which gave me the shock of my life. The trouble was he was always at the gate asking me to forgive him. It was easier to go back to him because I had nowhere else to go.

It was madness, I was besotted with him and we ended up on the streets when his mum kicked us out. I had been in and out of prison seven times for shoplifting and each time he would be waiting for me when I got out. I ended up as a prostitute in an effort to break his hold over me. That way I could sleep over at punters' homes and have a roof over my head for a while.

Finally when I reached 20, a really nice punter told me about a women's refuge place, so when I was last in court I told my solicitor I wanted a three-month sentence, so I could get off the shit and sort myself out. I went on methadone and when I got out, I went straight round to the refuge place and they took me in and fixed me up with my mentor, who really understands what I am going through.

I was free of him at last and started to sort myself out properly. My mentor has been great, as has everyone else who helped me, because it is almost impossible to do it on your own. You need a team around you. No one seems to understand how few places there are for women who want a fresh start, or the type of support and help we need to break away from bad men like mine.

I have got my own place now and no longer need to shoplift. I do slip back sometimes and smoke heroin, but always feel so guilty about it. I have a new partner who is a much better man than my last one. He knows that if he ever smokes heroin or hurts me, he will be out of my life!

... somewhere to go and someone to support you when you first come out of prison. Everyone who leaves prison should have access to a mentor like mine. I feel like a real citizen now and we are paying our bills. By next year, I want to be in college; and when I am over everything that has happened to me, I want to get a job. One day I would like to be a mentor, so I can help someone like me.'

Part 2 – April 2009

Claire is now 24 years old and... still in contact with her mentor: however they only meet every six months or so now. She is still in the same relationship and is proud of this, *'It has been good to be able to sustain a meaningful relationship for so long.'* She is also proud of other achievements, *'I have been drug free for 2 years now and am training to be a full-time Drug Worker... At the moment I am a voluntary worker and support drug addicts and sex workers. I go to College and have passed basic English and Maths tests. I am also receiving training in areas such as presentation skills, needle exchange, drug/alcohol abuse and risk assessments. There will be some full-time Drug Support Worker posts coming up and I plan to apply for one.'*

Claire has no doubts that her mentor and others have helped her get to where she is now, *'I could not have done it without them. My mentor and Drug Worker have been brilliant, and although it has taken over 4 years to get here I now feel normal – whatever that is! They have always been there for me and I will never forget them. Most recently I got support filling applications forms to begin Drug Support Worker training and had help preparing for the interviews. I would not have got this job without that support. Which is why I am doing what I am doing now – I am putting something back.'* Asked what she has achieved since we last met Clare says, *'I am drug free. I don't commit crime. I have a lovely home, which I am proud of. I have a job. I am in a stable relationship and I feel good.'*

(Wider Impact Consultancy 2009, unpublished)

Participatory activities

By participatory activities we mean using tools that involve the client in the evaluation or assessment process in an active way. These varied methods allow more creative and imaginative ways of obtaining feedback from your users than questionnaires and can be more enjoyable for the user. These mean that you do not have to use 'boring' surveys every time and some evaluation activities can be conducted with minimal reading and writing – or, indeed, without asking those taking part to write at all. Such activities can be used to obtain participants' views on the programme and about the wider gains they have made and how they apply them elsewhere in their lives.

Tools that produce visual evidence either for individuals or for groups can be fun and satisfying to complete (Evaluation Support Scotland 2007). For example, in work with children, a simple rainbow or ladder picture can be used to display their post-it notes on what they learned or gained from the project. Symbols such as smiley faces are widely used and available in most word-processing software. Participants can be asked to draw something representing their feelings or their progress from the start of the programme. Respondents might place stars or stickers against a display sheet offering a choice of responses, sort or rank cards, put up their hands, complete a body map or choose a position on a big scale on the wall or laid out on the floor. Numerous ideas for such exercises can be found on the Web and in handbooks, and Appendix B offers starting points for suitable approaches.

Many organisations use 'The Blob Tree' image illustrated in Figure 8.1 to enable clients to articulate how they feel. This can be used at the beginning of an intervention and again at subsequent points, or used retrospectively. This image was devised specifically for use with people with poor literacy skills but can be used with all abilities. The participant chooses one of the 'blob' figures that they feel relates to their experience and tells or writes why they have chosen that figure.

Where evaluation work is conducted in groups it is important to warm up with enjoyable activities and to introduce the task carefully. The worker needs to try to reduce the risk of individuals being influenced by pressure

FIGURE 8.1: THE BLOB TREE
COPYRIGHT PIP WILSON, FROM 'GAMES WITHOUT FRONTIERS' ISBN: 0-551-01554-3.
PUBLISHED BY MARSHALL PICKERING IMPRINT OF HARPER COLLINS PUBLISHING. NOT TO BE
PUBLISHED WITHOUT PERMISSION FROM:- PIP@PIPWILSON.COM WWW.PIPWILSON.COM

from others and should encourage individual and diverse responses, perhaps by repeating questions to elicit additional contributions. The facilitator will often need to dig deeper with prompts to reach the outcome information. The most frequent responses will be about what people have enjoyed but questions about progress, new learning, abilities and skills, or difference in current feelings from the state at the start can all be useful in turning respondents' minds to outcomes.

One of the problems, however, in using participatory activities is the need to capture the 'product' (what is said, drawn, filmed or photographed) as the evidence of outcomes. Sessions can be lively and busy and it is important to decide in advance how to record what is produced, keep the material produced safely and 'pull off' the findings and evidence of outcomes soon after the activity. A pre-planned recording sheet can be invaluable, where you decide in advance how you will record date and time of activity and who is involved, as well as keep a record of who said what. Using participants' initials and a spider diagram of their contributions can work well. If resources allow, it can be helpful to have one worker running the activity and a colleague acting as scribe. Flip-chart responses, explanations of drawings, group comments and so on should be typed up as soon as possible after the exercise as it is most dispiriting to have to try to reconstruct the results when you can no longer remember much about the event and inaccuracies will inevitably creep in.

It is perfectly legitimate to write up the users' responses for them. Indeed, it is valuable to do so as so many of us talk in more detail than we write. A simple check, 'Have I got that right?' is advisable when reading what you have written back to ensure that you have not imposed your perception of what they said. You could try, for instance, using what are sometimes called the knowledge, skills, attitudes and feelings (KSAF) questions with a small group to elicit the ways they have benefited and what has changed (Comfort *et al.* 2006, pp.41–45). Ask people to talk to each other about what they know now (as a result of the programme), what they can do now that they could not do before, how they now see things in different ways, and how they now feel differently about things. Completing the ends of sentences – such as 'I know about…'; 'I know how to…'; 'I'm more likely to…'; 'I'm now better at…'; 'I feel more…' – works well with some groups. The group members could fill in flip charts, keep notes or return to the whole group and share their answers. The comments can be collated for a report or a display of the group's achievements.

It is possible to adapt activities so that evaluation can be embedded in the project programme rather than being an add-on towards the end. Likewise, some projects use assessment tools at the beginning and end of an intervention to indicate change and distance travelled. In these settings assessment and review fit into the work very naturally. Reviews usually involve a worker and service user working together so that perceptions are corroborated and outcomes mutually agreed. Assessments can be formal written forms but it is also possible to use diagrams and scales to provide measures of progress.

The 'outcomes wheel', 'star' or 'spidergram' is one such device. Here the scales are arranged as spokes of a wheel or star and one criterion or indicator of progress is marked against each scale depending on the nature of the intervention. The client marks or colours in the wheel to indicate their own assessment of their progress, selecting from the lowest score of 1 to the highest of 10. This can be done at the beginning and at the end of the programme and will give a score for each indicator of difference or gain. There can be reasons to review progress retrospectively – that is, to think back at the end to how one was at the beginning. And there is sometimes benefit in using scaling to apply a number to an indicator and recording the numbers rather than colouring in a place on a wheel. What is important is that the person undertaking the evaluation has the interests of the service user firmly in mind, together with a concern for the rigour of the data-gathering process. These techniques are described more fully in Comfort's account of participatory exercises (Comfort *et al.* 2006). The client's own assessment can be discussed in relation to the perceptions of the worker supporting them and any differences of view can be explored. Such interactive joint assessments take considerable time if there is a thorough discussion but this can be worth while as they can be used to assess priorities for action, set targets and mark achievement as well as producing measures of progress for evaluation purposes. Figure 8.2 illustrates an 'outcomes wheel' devised for catering students in a Further Education college to enable them to assess their own growth in confidence during a Foundation Learning Tier programme. Here the criteria chosen for the segments of the wheel follow the indicators of confidence developed for young people as described in Chapter 6.

One version of the outcomes star has been devised by Triangle Consulting and the London Housing Foundation and developed through practice at St Mungo's, a charity working mainly with rough sleepers. The St Mungo Star is available to download and may be used for measuring the soft outcomes that homeless people need to make on the journey towards stability (MacKeith, Burns and Graham 2008). In discussion with a worker at assessment meetings, the star is completed by the client to mark their view of their position on a range of indicators. In respect of homelessness the indicators used are the factors that need to change in order to achieve

A score of 1 on the scales is the lowest and 10 is the highest and most positive.

Now I am this confident...

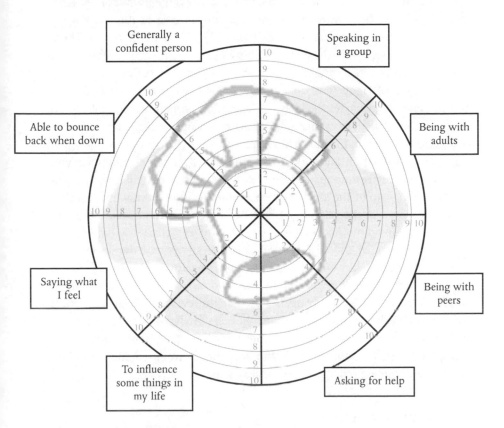

FIGURE 8.2: CONFIDENCE OUTCOMES WHEEL

independent and stable accommodation, such as managing money, self-care and living skills or reducing drug and alcohol misuse. Guidance is given on what each level on the scale means for each indicator. This is often used at the start to get a baseline and then later on during the programme or at its end. The indicators are arranged like the spokes of a wheel, on which the possible scores are shown. If the scores on each indicator are joined up, it will depict a star shape. If a client has improved their score on various indicators, the shape of the star changes. The product is therefore a visual representation of the client's progress as the points of their personal 'star' when they started the programme and at the later stage. Similar formats are now available for other fields such as work on alcohol misuse, mental-health recovery, employment, work in prisons and work with older people.

The homelessness star can be used to produce quantitative information on the progress of a group of clients. You should, however, be aware that *unless* the criteria for the scales on which people assess themselves are *precisely defined* and have been *tested and validated* (as in the case of the St Mungo's star), then such outcome stars or wheels are only a form of self-report. These can be used to report on the picture of how clients perceive and report their own progress but they cannot be used to derive valid statistical measures.

A degree of rigour and consistency in how we run the activities we use to generate evaluation evidence is essential. So before you embark on designing eye-catching evaluation formats or group exercises, remember to look back at your indicators. Those are the aspects of progress on which you need information and your tools should reflect them: otherwise you will generate interesting material but little in the way of evidence that you can use. Be aware of the sampling considerations also: as well as recording who is involved in the activity you need to find opportunities for anybody from the group who is not present at the activity to give their views. All the responses generated should be included in the analysis of the results; it is important not to select only the interesting or positive evidence. If we use an evaluation tool that requires a 'before' and 'after' response, it is critical to ensure that both stages happen and that the evidence from the first is available with the second at the point they are analysed. The second stage can be all too easily forgotten or earlier data lost. You should always give transparent details of the methods and approaches you used and should be careful to designate self-report responses as such.

Users' own material

Drawings, cartoons, poems, stories, letters, photographs or video diaries produced by project users can sometimes be used for evaluation purposes if they illustrate the progress made in some way. Such examples can make the text of a report more interesting and may offer insights into the day-to-day situations of those who come to us for help or increase the understanding of our partners of the way we work.

As always there are points of caution to bear in mind when considering the use of the client's own expressive material. Store such material carefully – a box full of unlabelled drawings or poems is of no practical use. The person themselves must give express permission for its use and should have an informed understanding of how their work will be used. Unless the client has given consent to the disclosure of their identity, it is important to make every effort to ensure anonymity. Even then pictures or details in the work may identify them and particular care should be taken when using the work of children or adults who are vulnerable.

It is important to provide enough information about the context for the reader to make sense of the material. It is crucial to understand creative work from the point of view of the artist and not to attribute our own understanding of its meaning. It is possible, for instance, to ask people to write some words to explain their picture or talk to you about it so that you can use direct quotations about the way they understand it. Pictures or similar material should be used where possible alongside other evidence that triangulates the user's description of progress.

Practice example

Spurgeons Beyond the Horizon is a service offering counselling for children on bereavement and loss, where children have lost a parent, sibling or other relative or where parents have separated or divorced. Spurgeons is one of the UK's largest Christian charities working with children, young people and families with projects in the UK and overseas.

This project has not escaped the pressure to show evidence of its outcomes but has had to develop its own approaches as there are obvious sensitivities involved and some of the children are very young. The counsellors use varied methods to help the children deal with their feelings about loss such as making memory boxes, doing a balloon release, creative activities such as making a candle or writing a poem, or joint activity days with other bereaved families. Numbers are relatively small in an intensive one-to-one intervention so it is possible for the counsellors to integrate evaluation work in their sessions to help the children express their feelings and recognise their own progress. 'The Blob Tree', for instance, is used to good effect to help clients articulate how they felt at the start of counselling and how they have felt as it progressed.

The organisation has developed its own simple evaluation form for under-14s. It allows the child to write and/or offer their own drawings and it asks one satisfaction question – 'Please draw or tell us what didn't help you' and one clear outcome question – 'Please draw or tell us what has changed for you'. A girl of seven who witnessed her father stabbing her mother wrote 'All the sadness is gone.' A six year old drew a picture of himself and his mother (illustrated below) and wrote 'I am happy now. My mom is happy now.' He then drew his finger puppet with the comment 'I tell my worries to it and it helps with my dreams about mommy and daddy.' The service then uses the evaluation forms to improve on things the children did not find helpful, show how many children can express some positive outcome and illustrate their comments. The drawings can also accompany case studies.

Another child was seven when her father committed suicide. She expressed her gains in an interview. 'I gave myself zeros at the beginning' she said 'because every time I looked at a picture of Daddy, I got upset but the counselling made me feel better and now I can talk about him without crying all the time.' However simply expressed, these things are outcomes in the children's own words.

Please draw or tell us what has changed for you:

The uses and abuses of qualitative material

Qualitative and self-reported information is essential to a rounded outcome evaluation. It helps to describe the factors behind the changes and benefits. It illuminates the needs of the clients as well as methods that have worked in enabling them to progress. It can help to evidence the soft outcomes that are harder to measure. It may fire the imagination and sympathies of funders in a way that quantitative data will not. Qualitative material may also provide a voice for the users either as individuals or collectively and articulate the meanings they attach to what has happened.

However, qualitative evidence can also be abused. If you are working with the personal comments, feelings and creative work of your users for evaluation purposes then you should take particular care to report it ethically and rigorously (see Denscombe 2005, pp.273–283), bearing the following in mind.

- The data is almost certainly not fully representative. Claims that the views or feelings expressed apply to the whole client group should be avoided.

- Data that does not fit the pattern, criticisms or alternative perceptions should also be portrayed in the report. It is extremely bad practice to select only the most positive comments or to depend on one case study that had exceptionally good outcomes. It is preferable to offer some measure of the proportion of users who had experienced the positive outcomes as well as their comments.

- Clients should not be exploited or subjected to any pressure to contribute their experiences.

- Salacious or intimate detail, or anything else that would embarrass the client should not be included.

- Anonymity should be preserved as far as possible.

- Your own values and feelings will affect how you view the material and may, in turn, influence the contributor. You should be aware of your own responses and double check with the user that you have correctly understood their interpretation.

- If you are coding for themes, you should not oversimplify to the degree that the original richness of the meaning is lost.

- Qualitative examples should be put in the context of how they were produced and selected. Quotations from clients should not be used out of context.

Do not use these qualitative methods without thinking through the practicalities for your own working context. You will frequently need to tailor tools and exercises yourself in order to reflect the outcomes you are seeking to produce and the needs, abilities and interests of your users. A light touch is necessary to put your users at ease and help them to contribute. It is often worth rehearsing to make sure you can give a clear introduction to the exercise and take good records of what is produced. Used with skill and discretion, these qualitative techniques can produce first-class evidence to enhance your evaluation.

CHAPTER 9

Analysing and Presenting Your Findings

Having decided what your outcomes are, what measures and indicators you will use and having collected that data, you will eventually reach the stage of writing up your findings. This chapter offers some guidance on how to analyse the data you have gathered and how to present the findings in an effective report. We also discuss how to make the best strategic use of your report on behalf of your agency, so that all the work of evaluation is used to maximum effect.

Interpreting survey data

It is far easier to start asking questions than to deal with analysing the answers! In Chapter 6, we urged you not to embark on designing questionnaires or other information-gathering methods without first considering what outcomes you need to evidence and what indicators you are going to use for those outcomes. You will also have piloted your survey or other instruments and will now have more precise ideas on how you intend to analyse the data. If you have completed that process thoroughly then analysis of responses becomes a great deal easier.

Clearly every questionnaire varies in its content but here are some general points on how to manage and present your findings on quantitative measures.

- Your information needs to be systematically recorded for all those questions you intend to analyse. You can do this on a manual summary sheet, on a computer spreadsheet or on a more sophisticated data-analysis package.

- In any case you should give each questionnaire its own reference number. This can indicate particular characteristics such as male or female (as in reference 001/F and 002/M) or you can record or code those characteristics separately. The key issues are that the answers of every respondent must be entered up and that you should be able to trace each answer back to the individual questionnaire for checking purposes.

- All the answers need to be counted. You may do this by, for example, ticking a column on the summary sheet. Figure 9.1 shows a simple summary-sheet format adapted from Bell's advice on how to analyse your data (Bell 1987, pp.103–123).

- If you have more than about 20 questionnaires, it may be best to put the answers onto a spreadsheet. A spreadsheet is in effect the same as a summary sheet, so this would look very similar whether you were analysing the answers using a computer spreadsheet or in a handwritten worksheet.

- On a spreadsheet you can enter words like 'Yes' or 'No' or 'Not known'. You can also code the answers by giving them a number, particularly where there are several different options (e.g. Yes = 1, No = 2, Not known – 3, Not answered – 4). Remember to allow a code for every option including unclear answers or no response or those that cannot be numerically correct (such as a child putting their date of birth as 1959). On a spreadsheet each possible response to a question or variable usually occupies one column. You can then either use the 'Count If' function to put the total at the bottom of each column, or programme in the formula for adding the totals in the columns.

- Begin to make sense of your material by grouping relevant data and looking at the totals (the frequencies of each factor). Why are some things more frequent than others? Is this accidental or is there a cause or a trend? (Denscombe 2005, pp.239–241.)

- Test your spreadsheet after entering up the data for a handful of questionnaires. Check that the categories or codes cover the full range of possible responses. Try some calculations and make sure that the resulting figures will give you the categories and information you need for your report.

- The days of using rulers and protractors to produce graphs and charts are virtually gone now. Spreadsheet programmes will produce charts automatically once the data and the totals have been entered

Summary sheet

Three questions from a survey in a training agency are taken here as examples of how to analyse using a simple summary sheet. The questions are as follows:

Please tick the answer in each case which applies to you.

1. Have you used the Second Chance Employment Project in the last six months?   Yes ☐   No ☐

2. What is your age group?:   16 – 25   ☐
                                                        26 – 35   ☐
                                                        36 – 45   ☐
                                                        46 or over   ☐

3. 'I feel my confidence to apply for jobs has increased as a result of using Second Chance.' Please circle one number on the scale below that shows your view about this statement.

Strongly disagree	Disagree	Neither agree nor disagree	Agree	Strongly agree
1	2	3	4	5

If you needed to analyse the answers to these questions, the summary sheet for counting responses could look like this. You would put 1 or a tick under the answer made by each respondent. When you have entered all the responses, the totals can be counted and used to create charts or report summaries.

Respondent reference no.	Question 1		Question 2				Question 3				
	Yes	No	16-25	26-35	36-45	46 or over	1	2	3	4	5
001	1			1							1
002		1				1		1			
003	1		1						1		
004	1			1							1
etc.											
Totals	3	1	1	2	0	1	0	1	1	0	2

FIGURE 9.1: A SIMPLE SUMMARY-SHEET FORMAT

up. On the best-known software, you use the Chart Wizard. Simply highlight the data with the titles for each category, choose the format you want (such as a bar or pie chart) and click so that the diagram appears in your spreadsheet.

- Always provide a title for tables, diagrams or charts and support them with an explanation in words of what the results mean. 'The task facing the researcher is to use these facilities to present the data in a way which is clear, precise and informative… As far as tables and charts are concerned, simplicity is a virtue.' (Denscombe 2005, p.242)

- You need to become familiar with basic spreadsheet functions and how to produce charts or have another colleague in your team who is practised in doing this. Remember that there is usually a 'Help' button. Type in a brief description of what you want to do (such as calculate the average or work out the median of the figures in a column), click on 'Search' or 'Go' and the programme will tell you which function to use.

- If you have a very large sample and need to produce statistical measures, such as the correlations between two factors, then you will almost certainly need to code your data and use one of the computer packages like SPSS (Statistical Package for the Social Sciences). You may well need assistance to use programmes like these.

- Consistency is the key to data input. *All* your responses must be entered and your system or codes should be rigorously followed. It is worth checking, say, 10 per cent of the entries to be sure that the input is accurate.

Once you have entered your data and have the broad totals of the different categories, you need to look for the trends and key facts you want to report. Look for what the figures tell you. What is their significance? What trends stand out? What are the most frequent responses? What are the averages? What is the evidence on whether outcomes were achieved or not? Where there are multiple-choice questions in a survey, it can be useful to look at what areas had the highest/most positive responses and which the lowest/most negative ones.

When you have decided which results are most relevant and important, you could then present the answers to particular questions in prose or use some tables or charts to break up the text and give it more interest and visual appeal. To provide a rounded picture, you should aim to show both the absolute number for a particular result *and* the percentage or proportion it represents. (For example, 17 adults learners out of a group of 20 gaining their OCN Level 2 certificate is a very good outcome but if it were 10 out of 100 that would tell a rather different story.) You should give an account of any negative results and not solely the positive story. As mentioned earlier, your report needs to detail the way in which you took any samples. You should also include details on how well the questionnaire operated, for instance, the characteristics of those who declined to respond and the difference made by non-response rates. A particularly important group of users may, for instance, have failed to respond or a poor overall return may make the findings less valid. If you can, do use some qualitative comments to help bring the figures to life.

Practice example

The Wildside Activity Centre provides adventurous and environmental activities for children and young people. In Chapter 3, we described the efforts made by the staff and Trustees to identify clear outcomes and begin the process of establishing evaluation systems.

By 2008/9, the Centre was using two evaluation forms – one for the children who had taken part in activities and another for teachers using the activities as part of the school curriculum. In addition, evidence was sought from the volunteers and young adult participants on their gains in social skills and qualifications.

The children's form showed animal figures asking open questions such as 'What did you do on your activity?' or 'What did you learn about the environment?' All the answers were completed in free text in the boxes provided. This posed a problem when potentially hundreds of forms had to be analysed as these answers needed to be categorised in some way.

The staff devised a coding structure so that data could be entered on a spreadsheet. For example, each activity offered was given a code (e.g. mountain biking = 1; pond dipping = 2; treasure hunt = 3). Answers about whether the children had learned anything on environmental matters were coded: Yes = 1, No = 2, No response = 3, Unclear = 4 and then Offered an example = 1, Did not offer an example = 2. The actual examples given were examined to see where the learning was occurring in themes such as the plants and animals observed, or the damage caused by litter, or the need to recycle, and so on. Quotations for use in the report could then be selected to illustrate those themes.

Please tell us about your visit to Wildside!

Age:………   **Date**:………

What did you do on your activity?

1.

Analysing qualitative data

As you will be aware from earlier chapters, interviews, participative exercises and many other evaluation methods can all yield qualitative evidence. You may be writing up a report from the transcribed notes of face-to-face interviews, replaying a video or using the free text comments of respondents to a written questionnaire. This is all likely to be chaotic information as most people do not think logically or answer questions precisely. There are sophisticated software programmes and research methods for analysing the content of written material but these will usually be beyond the scope of the typical evaluation in a community project. In any case, the evaluator must decide what words or themes to look for in order to set up such programmes. Here is some guidance that may help you. Bear in mind that they are only examples and you may, quite validly, choose a different way to make sense of your material.

- Give each respondent a reference number. Their comments may be recorded on a tape or video or in notes of an interview or exercise. Put the reference number on these documents.

- Read through a sample of your interview records or other responses. Look for the patterns and themes. Ask yourself 'What does this tell us?'

- If you have planned your evaluation thoroughly, you should ideally already know what indicators you are looking for. You could also select some key themes that are coming through from the interview notes or recordings.

- You then go through each set of interview notes and categorise or group the responses. You are looking for the recurring topics that relate to the purposes of your evaluation, especially those that show evidence of positive outcomes in the lives of service users.

- Find someone to give you a second opinion about how far your categories make sense and are likely to give you evidence on the central issues.

- Once you know what you are looking for, there are different ways of analysing the data depending on how much information you have to sift. They include making a grid or summary sheet similar to the one in Figure 9.1 or grouping similar comments together using 'cut and paste' or writing them out on flip charts or post-its (Evaluation Support Scotland 2009). A highlighter pen is useful (or different colours for different themes) and this may be quite sufficient for a small number of interview records. With a larger number of responses you may need to type them into a spreadsheet and code for your themes. The process is similar for analysing audio-visual material.

- Work out at least the approximate frequency with which each theme recurs. You could count for each category and present a bar chart (such as, the numbers of young mothers in a group mentioning feeling less isolated, being less depressed, or feeling more confident about establishing positive patterns of behaviour with their children).

- You could also count the numbers achieving positive change from their own perspective.

- Look for the relationships between factors. For example, does a particular activity show up more positive outcomes than others, or is one specific group of users falling behind.

- It is important to go back through the material and check that there are no other recurring patterns that you have missed. Make sure that you have reported a balanced picture and that there are no negative indications.

- If new and additional themes stand out, draw those out too. Notice the echoes in the responses. (For example, if it becomes clear that mainly white residents took up the activities for the elderly and that minority ethnic groups did not attend and tended to feel excluded, then note that finding).

- It is very important to use qualitative quotations in the report to give the feel of what people said.

- When reading or listening and looking for quotes, keep a note of the reference number of the notes and the point where you found the material. It can take a long time to go back through the documents to find that gem of an expression you saw earlier on!

- Make sure the respondent cannot be identified by anything said in the report. If there is any danger of that then revisit how it is expressed. Express permission should be sought if anyone who responded is to be named.

Practice example

Beacon Council programmes promote good practice in local government. The Beacon Councils' Positive Youth Engagement Programme was designed to address the Russell Commission recommendations to encourage youth volunteering within public services and to maximise the opportunities to involve young people in shaping local services and as active citizens in democracy. In the second phase of the programme, the original eight Beacon Councils supported 15 other authorities to develop such good practice in their own areas.

The evaluation of this 'peer support programme' investigated many aspects of the impact of the scheme including how far it had created new opportunities for volunteering and influencing public services and what benefits the young people had experienced. It also examined the barriers experienced to youth engagement, how they were overcome and the evidence of change in local services as a result.

Because each local authority was implementing the programme in different ways with different target groups of young people and no total list of participants existed, it was not possible to take a random sample of those involved. The young people's views were gathered through a semi-structured questionnaire distributed through the local authorities and also through a substantial number of individual interviews and focus groups.

The qualitative evidence of the focus groups was analysed mainly from the notes taken by the researchers. All the responses were typed out and then grouped for themes emerging.

At all the focus groups, the young people were asked *what they had gained* from the experience. Italics in the text below indicate the words used by young people themselves, either on flip charts or post-its or as recorded verbatim by the interviewer. By far the greatest level of response was about gains in confidence. A significant number of comments concerned gains in job skills and related experience, increased communication skills and teamwork, and making new friends. The findings of the study have been disseminated through a website to increase the spread of good practice and dialogue with other local authorities.

A few examples of young people's comments are set out below in relation to the main benefits they identified in the focus group discussions. The young people conveyed a strong sense that they saw themselves as giving service to others and took a pride in making a positive contribution, even though many ruefully pointed out how long it took for things to happen.

Gains in confidence

- *'I'm more confident and knowledgeable. What I have got out of this is more confidence with my speaking and I feel I am being heard and my world does mean something.'*

- *'I'm proud because of me confidence to talk to all the Councillors.'*

- *'Achieving things I wouldn't be able to achieve before.'*

- *'Not scared, maybe a bit wary. Before I went I didn't really know what a councillor was.'*

Improved social skills, making friends

- *'From coming here I have gained qualification in participation with young people and communications skills. Also I have gained security and friends.'*

- *'I've learned to think before I speak; be more diplomatic.'*

- *'And I hate talking in front of adults. But then* [the worker] *noticed and she got me to speak. Now I don't really mind.'*

Experience for CV, employment related skills and job search

- *'I have been able to gain other skills This is helping my CV and myself in the future and I have also met new people.'*

- *'To get an experience of real-life work.'*

- *'I can now be confident in an office environment. I can do all of what has been asked of me over the eight weeks.'*

- *'More life opportunities: it's made me like an entrepreneur.'*

Being able to make a positive contribution

- *'I've been able to make a positive contribution which will improve my immediate society* [in this borough]. *I've also learnt how to work as a team* [and] *got great training opportunities.'*

- *'Talking to Heads of Service and young people – useful skills for working with authority and young people.'*

- *'It causes changes in people – positive changes – it pushes you.'*

- *'When we were in care we didn't get our voice heard. We can see what we've missed out on. When we was in care there was no* [forum like this].*'*

In addition, the young people were asked to produce imaginary text messages to their friends telling them about what it was like being involved. These bring the benefits to life in the terms (however ungrammatical!) used by young people themselves.

- *Been involved in volunteering project – totally epic! Met loads of new people … Got tons of ideas for youth forum stuff and done volunteering qualification. Well worth getting into!*

- *OMG Hun! This volunteering fing is qyt gud! Lol I didn't fink itd be dis gud lol. U Shud try it owt!*

- *This… group is mint. It's cool meeting new ppl and stuff. It's a mint feelin being part and representing* [my borough].

- *Areet Waaz, I'm @* [Beacon group]. *Its well cushty we discover what places oru their r gd 4 yp. Nd which places aint. It's a great team I luv cumin ere.*

The individual interviews with young people produced ample confirmation of the main benefits of the schemes. Some of the examples they gave of what had happened to them showed subtle relationships between their improved self-image and how they fared in other contexts. In several cases, the young people could see that adults had changed their perceptions of them so that they were no longer so trapped in negative positions.

'I'd been getting into trouble in school and my head of year had been pointing in my face and making out I'm horrible and he called me "a horrible little dick". Yes – he swore at me and then I showed him this [his folder of

work] *and it shows I'm not horrible ...now he's dead canny to us, since I've shown him what I do.'* (Young person undertaking accreditation.)

(Hoggarth *et al.* 2009b)

Being clear about the evidence – some pitfalls in presenting data

There are some classic traps awaiting all report writers! We will remind you of some of the main issues here but you may also want to look back to the passages in Chapter 6 on the appropriate use of numerical data and in Chapter 8 on the abuses of qualitative material. Your aim must be to make as clear to the reader as possible what the findings actually mean. 'Spin' and mystification do not enhance the credibility of your evaluation. Typical mistakes in reporting evidence include the following:

• Reporting in a way that only highlights the positive. Contraindications and criticisms should be even-handedly reported but it can be helpful to explain the reasons for any problems and what steps are being taken to address them.

• Failing to identify clearly the sample used, how it was drawn and to what time period it applies.

• Not making clear how many people responded or benefited and the proportion these are of the whole group of potential respondents. (For example, if only 10 patients filled in evaluation forms out of 175, it is not sufficient to say that those responding felt that the treatment improved their condition. The response received does not give a picture of the whole group.) Best practice is to provide both the actual number and the proportion (for instance, '120 children out of 200 on the project (60 per cent) now have improved reading scores.'). Proportions and percentages help us interpret the significance of the raw numbers in the text.

• Exaggerating numbers or responses. When numbers are small, use actual numbers rather than percentages.

• Using self-reported responses as precise numerical measures. Self-reported scores are subjective and may not mean the same from one respondent to another, unless the system has been extensively tested for reliability (see Chapter 6).

• Offering generalisations without showing how the finding was arrived at from the figures.

- Making sweeping claims of proven cause and effect. It will only be extensive studies, probably using randomised control studies that can come close to showing statistical evidence of the causal link between a specific intervention and the impact on service users (see Chapter 2, 'Randomised control studies').

- Claims of cause and effect are in any case usually risky, as it is often difficult to isolate the effect of a single project's contributions to the outcomes from those made by the work of other partners. It is always good practice that partners should be acknowledged.

- Using long or technical words. If you need to use a technical term, try to explain it or just mention in brackets.

Try to be thorough, clear and honest about what you found. In the long run that will only foster the good reputation of your agency.

What makes a convincing report?

As discussed in Chapter 1, evaluation can have many different purposes. In this book we are chiefly concerned with the need to show evidence of results but, as we have touched upon, evaluation can be used both as you go along to improve the service you offer (formative evaluation) or at the end to make an assessment of how effective the service or programme has been (summative evaluation). Ideally schemes should undertake both types of evaluation.

Activity

Imagine that you are the Lead Commissioner in the local authority for your field of service provision. You probably receive dozens of evaluation reports in the course of your work.

This time you are considering a submission by a particular organisation for provision of a much-needed service. You have a recent evaluation report to hand on their work.

If you are to consider this agency as a serious candidate as a provider what will you need to know? What are you hoping this report will tell you? What will you look for in its style and presentation?

What do your answers to the questions above tell you about how evaluation reports need to be structured and presented?

The hallmarks of effective use of formative evaluation are chiefly:

- the inclusive consultation of users and other interested people during the evaluation
- clear evidence of adaptation in response to the recommendations
- the efforts made to give feedback to users.

Here, however, we are concentrating on the characteristics of a convincing summative (perhaps final) evaluation report. Appendix A offers a structure and sample headings to form a basis for your report. Put your plan down on paper early on, especially if you find writing difficult. Then you can begin to fill in the sections as you go along so it does not all pile up near the deadline. You can keep draft paragraphs on file on topics you will use repeatedly, such as the description of your agency and its services or the target outcomes for each of your funded programmes.

The following points may help you flesh out the structure of your report.

- The report should outline the nature of the organisation, its general mission and what it provides. You should give enough of a context to enable the reader to understand the approach and methods of the service in question.

- It may make general reference to current policy in relevant fields such as the targets of the national drugs strategy or the outcomes of *Every Child Matters* to put the objectives of the programme in context.

- A good report will tell the reader the answers to their questions about the scheme. It is worth reflecting on the questions your audience is likely to have and writing a summary which addresses those issues directly.

- It will describe the *desired outcomes* of the scheme and any particular targets that were agreed with the funding body.

- The report will describe the *methodology* (how the evaluation was conducted) and highlight any limitations. It will be precise about how representative the data is and what findings can be argued from it.

- The report will describe the *inputs* for the programme, including volunteering and in-kind contributions.

- It will set out the *outputs* achieved in quantitative terms (how many attended, how many sessions, how many people were trained, etc.)

- It will then summarise the evidence on *whether the intended outcomes were achieved or not.* This is likely to include both quantitative measures and qualitative descriptions of progress (e.g. case studies, or service users' accounts). It may offer evidence of 'soft outcomes' and perhaps the perspectives of stakeholders. It should give the reader a feel of how the outcomes are achieved. (You may want to revisit here the discussion in Chapter 6 on the types of evidence you should be offering to give a comprehensive picture).

- The report will say specifically whether the particular targets of the funding in question were met or not.

- If other outcomes were achieved that were not necessarily part of the original funding agreement, the report should elaborate on them. This may help to show the added value of the service or the breadth of its effectiveness.

- Evaluation reports will often deal with key *process issues,* especially where that was one of the original reasons for the study. They may draw attention to the barriers in the process of setting up or running the scheme that prevented full effectiveness, such as inadequate premises or weak governance.

- To reassure the audience, it is often useful to mention the key procedures that the scheme put in place (e.g. Were the staff and volunteers CRB checked if appropriate? Were risk assessments in place?).

- The report will ideally make an estimate of 'value for money'.

- It should show that formative evaluation was fully used and changes were made as a result.

- The report will be critical where necessary. An account of a perfect programme does not make for credible reading.

- It will not claim proven cause and effect unless in exceptional circumstances the necessary rigorous research methodology was used.

- The report will give due credit to partner agencies.

- Some recommendations for the future will normally be set out beyond simply continuation of funding. These will chiefly focus on how the scheme can improve year on year.

- It will mention key groups of non-users, discuss the reasons for this and whether changes are required for the future.

- If the report is a long one (say over about 15 to 20 pages), it will probably need an executive summary of the main points.

- Usually, a copy of the research tools used, such as questionnaires, should be included as appendices.

Your report should be readable and clear and should certainly not be boring. Tables, graphs or charts can help to enliven the text and make findings understandable. Quotations from users, creative work or photographs often help bring things to life. A report with poor spelling and grammar does not make your agency look professional: make sure your text is spell-checked and proofread.

Practice example

Women's Aid Leicestershire provides two refuges for women suffering domestic violence. It also offers outreach work and an Independent Domestic Violence Advice Service. It receives a substantial proportion of its funding from the Supporting People programme, which requires online submission of outcome data. This is reported in national summaries but is not made available for individual agencies.

Further means are needed of conveying the progress of the work to other partners and potential supporters. The annual report is the main vehicle for such information and is a model of interesting reading. It shows outputs such as numbers of users, the ethnic breakdown of users and the numbers of referrals in eye-catching graphs and pie charts. It portrays the outcomes for the women who use the refuges and are encouraged to make their own decisions about the next steps, which might include moving on to specialist hostels or supported housing, returning to a partner in reconciliation, or being rehoused into more permanent accommodation. It also uses quotations from service users and their creative writing. The work of the organisation is portrayed in a way that can be used to maximum strategic effect.

The women are encouraged to express themselves in various ways especially through poetry. This often shows the distance they have travelled. The poems below are written by three of the women who have suffered violence and abuse and are included with their permission. The women are invited to read their own work at a celebration of progress called SurviveHER Day held annually during Domestic Violence Week. They also contribute to the training of professionals and information sessions for potential funders.

1:
My aim was changing . . . ME
My look, my life, away to be !!
A space in time is what I'm given.
I'm ½ way there I intend to start living

2:
I'm with attitude!! was a bit misguided though!
I'm gonna use my attitude it'll make me flow!
I'm making plans, clear goals drive me on,
This is me, my essence!!

3:
I'm running away again got to start my life anew!
How will it all turn out? What am I to do?
Ideas are coming thick and fast, this refuge has me buzzing,
Join this, attend that, my confidence is soaring!
And now I'm in my own place, independent I shall be!
I must now share this vibe around and I'll do it voluntarily.

Using your report strategically

Too many evaluation reports absorb a great deal of effort in production and are then made little further use of once they have been submitted to the funding body. That may be just as well for low-quality and badly presented reports with poor evidence behind them but it is a waste in the case of a good report. As you start to plan – and, indeed, when you have finally finished – an evaluation report, give some thought to how you can best use it strategically to further the aims of your project. Although it may be sufficient to answer the requirements of your current funders or to make a case for new resources, a good report can also be used more widely.

Depending on the context of your service, you may like to consider some of the following possibilities:

- Evaluation reports can be sent to stakeholders, referring agencies, or potential donors.

- Think about mailing your reports to key decision-makers, including local politicians. They can be used to increase awareness of what the agency offers and its effectiveness.

- A report can help to give others a better insight into the situations that service users face and the ways in which they are helped to change things for the better.

- It may inform partners and potential funders about the effectiveness of specific methods used in the project.

- The whole report or sections of it can sometimes be attached to further funding applications: a reputation for effective work tends to snowball.

There are also other ways of increasing the publicity for positive outcomes beyond the evaluation report itself. A major report may deserve a launch event or may be given extra impetus through press releases, journals or academic articles. Some of the content may be useful for the project website or the whole report may be made available. The information may help in campaigns on gaps in services or the needs of particular groups. Quotations, short case examples or quantitative evidence of outcomes can all be used in future publicity or annual reports.

Practice example

Wirral Council has had a long-term policy of involving young people in decision-making and in the democratic processes of the local authority. Young people are involved through a number of inter-linked structures such as area youth forums, schools councils, advisory committees and an annual youth conference. They take real responsibility for allocating youth grants and directly advising Councillors and officers on youth issues such as the needs of young people in the care system or the commissioning procedures for the Children and Young People's Directorate. The young people gain from this experience, with evidence of greater self-confidence, better communication skills, increased ability to take responsibility and other new skills that can help them with job applications or college entry. The benefits to the Council include more responsive planning and, in the longer term, a reduction in the alienation of young people from voting and democratic systems. There is, however, a continuing task of developing youth engagement and embedding it in the Council's systems and values that requires commitment and resources.

In 2008, the young people suggested that swimming pools should be free to children and young people in the holiday periods and that this would reduce youth nuisance. The Councillors showed great faith in these young representatives and decided to implement the recommendation at a cost of £187,000 in four public swimming pools in areas with high levels of vandalism and crime. Key to the success of the venture was the careful evaluation of the results of the initiative.

Geographically coded police data on anti-social behaviour and criminal damage, information from Merseyside Fire and Rescue Service on fire setting, and information on youth nuisance incidents from the Wirral Community Patrol team were collated for the neighbourhoods around the pools. Trends for 2008/9 were compared with figures for the summer period in the previous year. One pool that did not have the free swimming initiative was also randomly selected as a 'control'. Early indications showed some encouraging reductions in anti-social behaviour in the neighbourhoods of the pools concerned, compared with the previous summer and compared with an increase in the neighbourhood of the 'control' pool that did not have free swimming.

The report was submitted to the relevant Council committees and was very well received, not only because of the provisional signs of successful outcomes but also because of the efforts made to evaluate the programme. The report was used strategically not just to make the case for holiday provision for young people but also to increase the confidence of the elected Members and senior officers across the Council in the value of engaging young people in service development. As one senior Councillor put it at interview with an evaluator *'From our point of view it has spin offs – definitely worthwhile.'*

(Staunton 2008, unpublished)

CHAPTER 10

The Pros and Cons of the Outcome Focus

Some advantages of concentrating on outcomes

The current emphasis on outcomes has huge potential to improve the quality of delivery to service users. It can help to sharpen our focus on the actual benefits to the client instead of allowing us to concentrate on the amount of work we do or the finance coming in to the organisation in grants or commissions. As we argued early on in this book, there is no excuse for empire-building: services are there to make a difference and to help their users. There is no justification for continuing to pour public or charitable funds indefinitely into ineffective schemes. This rationale by itself justifies the shift to the outcome focus.

'Outcome models' can help us in designing our programmes by highlighting effective interventions likely to achieve particular changes. Properly used, they can describe complex programmes with the contributions of different partners. They can show how the efforts of individuals, agencies, and whole services add up and fit together to achieve the change we want for a whole city or area. The needs analysis required and the accountability through continuing evaluation can help to drive the efforts of the many complex inter-agency partnerships that characterise public services today. In some circumstances, competition between agencies may be reduced with recognition of the different contributions to achievement of the same goals. In order to achieve major change at the population level, numerous partners and the local residents themselves have to contribute. Collaboration is not an end in itself; it is a means of achieving change in a complex situation.

What is important is the change achieved and not claiming causal effects for the work of a particular organisation.

Results-based accountability and logic models also make evaluation easier. They help 'logically' to plan the chain of steps needed and to check what happened at each stage. It makes evaluation much more focused because the intended outcomes have been clearly defined at the beginning of the process. Outcome evaluations make for better articulation of the mission and achievements of the agency and can increase the motivation of the staff and their understanding of their roles. For users and staff alike, they can bring a sense of reward and confidence from the documenting of progress.

Some reservations about logic models

We are not, however, unreasoning advocates of the outcome approach. Undoubtedly, it has its downsides and some of them may cause major problems for the future of our services. We summarise some of these knotty issues here.

The search for 'what works', for 'high-quality evidence' of successful interventions, inevitably shows up those programmes, often from America, that have been able to finance long-term control studies. Commissioning processes are starting with the changes to be achieved and will tend to use providers that can already show evidence of effectiveness. This may then lead to applying apparently effective programmes (which have been able to afford the research) in blanket fashion. The main problem with this seemingly blameless logic of using 'what works' is that it stifles innovation. Innovative approaches obviously cannot show a track record of successful outcomes because they are still new. The tendency is therefore to lean to the cautious conservative approach. Established methods are more likely to draw in the funding. There is much less room for trying things out and building on the lessons learned.

> I am very troubled by the movement to fund only research-proven practice. This movement's intent to take advantage of proven methods and make the best possible use of scarce dollars is laudable. But there are two problems. First, the research world does not have all the answers. There are many important and powerful ideas that have never been fully tested by research. If we fund only programs that have been tested, we cut ourselves off from these other ideas. Second, thinking beyond research is often the most creative edge of the work. We must allow for the development of new knowledge. I have no problem in giving preference to research, but we must also allow research to be

adapted to the unique circumstances of each community, and we must give people room to experiment and learn. (Friedman 2005, p.49)

Those who commission the use of existing programmes with what they see as 'proven' effectiveness often emphasise 'fidelity'. This means that the programme must be implemented exactly as it was designed. Where schemes are delivered differently through local adaptation or because of a lack of skills on the part of the staff, they can become ineffective. While this is certainly a problem it also raises other issues. The programme may be inappropriate in the first place for broad application to all groups or may fail to take particular local factors into account. For instance, there has been substantial research into the outcomes of programmes aiming to improve parenting skills and behaviour. The evidence for certain programmes is very convincing and they have often been widely adopted elsewhere with the requirement of fidelity. This may, however, miss certain cultural traditions or even economic influences in some communities and may result in apparently successful approaches being ineffective in those situations. In our view, care is also needed to ensure that effective community-based schemes and small organisations that do have the understanding of the local conditions are not lost in this process. The caution of the realist evaluators is important here – that we should look for 'what works *for whom and in what circumstances*' (our italics) not simply for 'what works' (Pawson and Tilley 1997). Interventions may work for some people but not others (and might even work *against* some people) and the circumstances under which the programme operates can be different in different agencies and situations.

The second major problem with outcome models is that organisations and professional workers will always chase targets. If the targets are framed as outcomes then that will shape the behaviour both of decision-makers and of the staff who work with the clients just as much as if the targets are defined as the quantity or outputs of the work. Workers may concentrate only on those areas of work that meet official targets. Sometimes targets are adjusted down to disguise a lack of performance. Worse still, people may cream off the lower risk cases and leave those with complex and multiple problems where it may not be so easy to show positive outcomes.

This does not in our view negate the necessity of identifying outcomes and assessing results but it has led many people to reject the outcome approach. A single-minded drive to achieve any target will exclude other needs and can prevent the use of other beneficial interventions. People will 'teach to the test'. In other words, they seek to meet the indicators and criteria of success even if that does not ultimately meet the needs of the service users or offer them real benefit. Sometimes participants are channelled into certain training or treatments because such measures are likely to satisfy particular targets. Critics argue that targets, including outcome targets, are therefore not in the long-term interests of the clients and may stifle personal development because they narrow the choice of areas to work on and the options for interventions. Hard outcomes come in for particular venom because they are seen as failing to recognise the small steps of progress, the soft outcomes, that are usually necessary to achieve them. We do not go as far as this wholesale rejection of outcome targets but we do recognise that a blinkered focus on set outcomes is highly unlikely to help people or communities facing major deprivation or multiple problems. Some flexibility, recognition of distance travelled and valuing of the wider incidental outcomes of a programme are required. The perspectives of different vocational disciplines may also need to be recognised.

Those whose performance is under scrutiny using outcome models can be driven to fudge results. If the definitions of what counts towards achievement are not tight, people will naturally tend to reckon anything marginal as a positive outcome. Often the outcomes put forward will be constructed so that the agency is certain they can be achieved: the temptation is not to risk stretching for better performance as funding may be put at risk. Outcome information can also be used out of context (Rossi, Lipsey and Freeman 2004, p.227). A typical example would be the reporting of figures about workless people entering training or jobs. In some cases, the headline results are reported without reference to the 'churn' factor – that is, how long those people stay in a job or on a course and how often they re-enter the benefit system. The outcome is very different if somebody stays in employment for two years as opposed to staying for two weeks but depending on how the indicators are framed both could count as a positive outcome. In order to assist a proper interpretation of the figures, the reporting should describe the context such as the local economic situation, the type of clients and the average length of stay in employment.

In any case, some people would argue, the emphasis on channelling funding almost solely into the achievement of outcomes determined by governmental or quasi-governmental bodies jeopardises minority interests and the independence of the voluntary sector. Faith groups and other bodies which for ethical or religious reasons want a measure of distance from State control are not infrequently forced to choose between diluting their mission and applying for public funding. Where the specialist need they exist to meet is not yet recognised in the planning cycles, other bodies may be placed in the same position. There is still a place for genuinely independent voluntary effort that meets need and fills serious gaps, despite the financial pressures that will mean for those attempting to preserve such work.

Logic models can become 'top down'. Senior people at the 'centre' (for example, of a local authority or government department) are often charged with assessing needs from statistical evidence and deciding what outcomes should be priority. The process may take a long time but it may still miss important needs, especially of minorities or less visible groups. Consultation with local people or groups in particular need may be perfunctory or non-existent. It is clearly impossible to include everything that needs improving but this can leave some very worthwhile projects without an obvious link to the chosen outcomes. The centralised planning method can find itself at odds with other trends towards local devolution and more involvement of local people in democratic planning processes. It is also clear that it can leave a wide gap between the strategic planning process and the staff at fieldwork level who have to deliver the outcomes. There is a major communication issue and many community projects may simply not catch up with the key planning processes and the desired outcomes until it is too late. As mentioned in earlier chapters, it is not uncommon for fieldwork staff to be unaware of the outcomes they are supposed to be achieving and many will have no understanding of how they have been arrived at or, indeed, may never have heard of an outcome model.

Logic modelling does not deal well with issues of power, control and conflict. It is based on the idea that 'interventions' will change something for the (largely passive) 'target group'. It focuses most on outcomes determined through the planning process and is largely silent on issues of what happens if people do not agree their importance. Hence it is not easy to incorporate active participation of service users in the process, and this is counter-productive because, as any good fieldworker will tell you, the user needs to be engaged and committed, genuinely wanting the changes in their own life in order to derive maximum benefit from any programme. Communities need to sign up to what will be entailed in achieving significant improvements or the efforts will be steadily undermined.

There is a hidden trap in the supposed rationality of the process. Not only can consultation be inadequate but logic models, particularly when explained by over-enthusiastic fans, can sound as if they confer omnipotence. It is too easy to believe that because there is a careful plan with all the required elements, it can and must succeed in delivering the outcomes. If the details of the needs assessment, the research used to support the choice of 'evidence-based' methods or the basic assumptions of the planning model are wrong or misleading in the first place, it can take a very long time for this to become apparent. There may be a need to adapt programmes as they are implemented to suit local conditions or adjust for new factors emerging or past errors in the planning process. The corporate planning process may, however, have become a juggernaut, ploughing on unstoppably in the name of logic.

Logic models tend to focus on a single result or a small number of outcomes at a time. This can oversimplify the picture and fail to take account of unintended consequences, though every intervention has its side-effects. They tend to treat the process as a chain of consequences – from intervention to outcome – where each stage must be completed, whereas in reality change occurs through a complex network of different influences and not necessarily by a logical sequence of steps. Logic models tend to pay less attention to the importance of processes in organisations, as if the intervention will work automatically regardless of how it is implemented or managed. In practice, it is often the small details of inter-personal relationships, the way in which partnerships work or do not work, or the unforeseen facts in the process of implementation that derail achievement. The plan itself does not guarantee success.

Problems in assessing outcomes

Because of this complexity, it is often difficult to demonstrate a clear connection between inputs, outputs and outcomes. We may not know the precise link between activity and outcome or how exactly a set of inputs and activities leads to particular outcomes. We wish to see a simple cause and effect but this is very rarely possible in practice. It is possible, for instance, that youth nuisance has reduced because of a particularly wet summer rather than because of police initiatives or summer play-schemes. In the reverse case, burglary figures could be rising on account of economic conditions, despite an effective crime-prevention scheme. Small projects are unlikely to achieve major changes on their own and even large organisations use a network of partners and benefit from other related changes in social conditions.

Many of the problems with assessment lie in the accuracy of the evaluation design. If the indicators used are badly framed, they will show up false or inaccurate trends on outcomes. They can also distort practice. There needs to be a solid justification that the measures chosen do have a relationship to the outcome in view and that working to demonstrate them will not have a negative effect on the overall benefits for the service users. Too much significance can be ascribed to the results from one method, such as one particular questionnaire or scaled test. This makes another reason for advocating the use of multiple measures and the use of both qualitative and quantitative approaches.

Some of the outcomes we aim to produce are by nature hard to define. Healthy lifestyles or a high level of social cohesion in a community, or self-esteem, resilience or emotional wellbeing for individuals are all highly desirable but difficult to pin down. Many, if not most, of the outcomes we most desire in our lives are equally intangible and it almost always takes many smaller achievements to build the most valuable impacts. In the face of the problems of measurement across different providers, the authorities may sometimes impose inappropriate standard measures. Accepting these difficulties does not make us shy away from the effort to evaluate progress on such factors. We can acknowledge the problems of assessment and strive for high quality and transparent methods while continuing the endeavour to find good ways of evidencing the very sorts of outcomes we find most valuable. In an article about measuring impact of voluntary sector work on children's wellbeing, Neville and Keen (2009), writing for the charity New Philanthropy Capital, argue that:

> Charities need to put more effort into measuring feelings, in order to prove the full impact of their work. If charities do not fully measure their impact, they can't tell you what is effective. This means that the most effective approaches cannot be scaled up, the least effective approaches cannot be challenged and the maximum benefit for children cannot be achieved. (Neville and Keen 2009, p.8)

The logistics of commissioning

The concept of what commissioning entails and the working understanding of how to go about it are still developing and planning cycles do not always flow smoothly. This can present a number of problems for delivery on the ground.

- The length of time required for needs analysis and decision-making in the partnership bodies responsible makes the process unwieldy. It is difficult to respond fast to anything, even an urgent new need.

- Evaluation of impact necessarily takes even longer. We may not know until it is too late that the commissioning decisions were never going to produce the intended effects.

- Clear identification of need depends on the methods and accuracy of the needs audit and the information it takes into account. If this stage is not completed thoroughly, the decisions about priorities will be shaky. The political process may also sideline some issues despite an obvious case for need.

- In practical terms, because the processes are relatively new in many situations, decisions are currently often not known until very late in a financial year. This places enormous stress on organisations waiting to know if their work will receive new or continued support. Cash-flow crises can result for some.

- Although there is a requirement to show evidence of outcomes at the end of the planning cycle, there is not always time for organisations to produce adequate evaluation especially where one- or two-year funding is approved. There may also be insufficient time to absorb the findings of evaluations while the commissioning process moves on.

- The outcome models developed for commissioning purposes tend to concentrate on producing results at population level, changes for the whole community. It is often difficult to trace a link between these major changes for a population and the interventions chosen for funding. Although the planning cycle is portrayed as being logical and rational, it may in fact be more *ad hoc* and approximate than is usually admitted.

Problems facing small organisations

As mentioned earlier, the tendency to fund programmes on the basis of quantifiable measures and evidence-based work can leave small agencies struggling. They are unlikely to have been able to produce major evaluations, let alone long-term case control studies of the effectiveness of their interventions. Few funding regimes allow an adequate proportion of awards to be devoted to evaluation and some do not support the evaluation element at all. External studies are therefore usually well beyond the reach of many community-based organisations.

Even if projects are well informed and working well to the intended outcomes, they are still 'on their own' as the logic model does not tell them how to evaluate their outcomes and demonstrate effectiveness. They may still be at a disadvantage at the stage where evidence of outcomes is demanded. Many do not have staff with the necessary skills and experience to undertake evaluation and inevitably in a small organisation, the task is an additional responsibility on top of the pressures of work with service users.

Overall the trend does seem to militate against smaller organisations. There are some concerns being voiced over the impact being felt, especially in the voluntary sector. We have no ready answers to these questions but we have observed some success where organisations have banded together to cope. It is possible, for instance, to organise the work through a federation or syndicate of agencies, where the collective seeks and is accountable for the funding. We have also seen examples of projects with similar aims and methods sharing evaluation, for instance, in mentoring programmes or community-based sports schemes. This has enabled a small contribution in cash or kind from each project to support a more substantial study. Where the measures and indicators are agreed and shared, the findings can be aggregated to show a wider and more convincing pattern of impact.

Revisiting the benefits

Some of these difficulties can be lessened if a truly broad range of people are involved and consulted in choosing the outcomes and methods of intervention and if the complexity of change is recognised. Methods of evaluation need to be of high quality and operated with integrity. Commissioners and managers need to develop a greater appreciation of the effect of the planning cycles on those delivering services and foster much better communication with those on the ground.

Although we have acknowledged the problems of outcome modelling here, we return now to emphasising its advantages. Outcome and performance accountability models can be very powerful planning tools. They sharpen the focus of evaluation effort. Fundamental to their usefulness is that they demand we look at the actual effect of our programmes rather than at our need to justify and continue them. They are focused on the benefit to the user not on the benefit to the organisation or those that work in it. They then offer a 'logical' way of planning for what we want to achieve. Above all, they can help to hold the different players to account for the results.

Conclusion

So get started!

We end where we began. We used the first part of this book trying to persuade you that, whether you like it or not, those who fund services working with people whether through grants or commissioning processes now tend to plan their programmes and distribute resources in order to achieve particular chosen outcomes. Not only are they determined to see a difference in the lives of service users and local communities but they consciously prioritise those changes that seem most necessary and urgent. It follows that the search for evidence of outcomes is now an integral part of work in public services. Evaluation becomes an indispensable requirement not an added extra. Survival of our organisations can depend upon it. We need credible evidence of the results of our work not just the quantity of effort.

We hope that by now you have some of the know-how and tools that will enable you to make a good start and that we have convinced you of the need to absorb the implications of the outcome emphasis into your own practice.

So, do it! Act on the conviction and get started. It does not matter if you feel you will not get it perfectly right or that there are still things you do not understand. If it has not happened to you already, it will not be long before you need to produce some evidence of the effectiveness of your work. The best evaluation schemes are embedded in the day-to-day work of an agency but that takes time and many adjustments along the way. You can only build an appropriate evaluation system by starting somewhere. Use the advice we have provided to help you plan and implement your evaluation consistently but do not use planning as a reason for delay. Start somewhere to gather some evidence of the positive difference your scheme makes and build on it.

It may have unexpected benefits

When you do make a start on developing a consistent evaluation system geared to collecting and analysing the evidence you can show for the outcomes of your work, it may surprise you how much it benefits your organisation. It is not wasted effort: the dividends can be enormous. They may well include better communication between managers and other staff and greater job satisfaction as workers see in print the evidence of the difference they make. It will probably influence your planning processes for the better. You may have more fruitful dialogue with funders and commissioners and should experience fewer crises over funding. You will gain new skills in data gathering and analysis and the pool of evidence will grow as you go along. It will enable all concerned to articulate the purpose of the work and the impact it makes. The focus on making a real difference will benefit service users and they will appreciate the feedback on their own progress and the improvements to provision.

Whatever the problems – evidence of outcomes is a necessity

This book is not a theoretical text comparing results-based accountability, outcome programmes and logic models. The average reader may therefore have breathed a sigh of relief but some may feel that we have glossed over the differences between the many different approaches to planning for outcomes. Undoubtedly some models are more flexible and responsive than others and public bodies engaging in commissioning on an outcome model will choose the one that suits their situation.

We do not want to dwell on this. For most organisations engaged in service delivery, the impact of these models has been clearly felt in their day-to-day work. We do not believe that the emphasis on outcomes will go away. However, we do see some trends towards the introduction of standardised evaluation systems for particular types of service or intervention. Probably as a result of some of the difficulties in assessing outcomes, some services are being brigaded into groups with common measures or national indicators and sometimes online returns.

For most organisations this will not remove the necessity for an evaluation process of their own. Some may be serving a specialist function, not easily picked up in the broad analysis of need. Most agencies will have multiple sources of funding or will need to diversify to help ensure their sustainability. Qualitative evidence is needed to reinforce quantitative measures. Only by having a system for collecting outcome evidence on a regular basis across a range of indicators and through using a variety of methods, can you be ready for the next grant application or the next review.

We have written this book to contribute to giving the best work with people a proper profile. There are workers who have flare and imagination, who innovate, who care deeply about the users of their service, and who are totally committed to bringing about positive change where it is most needed. We do not want to see such projects go by the board because they could not evidence their outcomes. We want this work to have the best chance of survival.

It is important not to deify the outcome plan itself: what matters is the difference it achieves for individuals and communities. If it is applied with common sense, in a measured and flexible way, outcome planning has a huge potential for improving services and changing the quality of life. If you fail to take account of the trend towards demands for evidence of the outcomes of your work, it is more than likely that your project will not be around to influence how these processes develop in the future. We do not believe that this movement is a flash in the pan. Use it to advantage now.

Examples and Checklists to Help You

In this appendix we offer:

    a) an example of an introduction of an evaluation to the respondent

    b) an example of a consent form

    c) a format for an evaluation plan

    d) recommended headings for an evaluation report.

A. An outline introduction to an evaluation for respondents (to be adapted as appropriate)

[Name of evaluators]

Evaluation of [name of study]

Information for respondents

WHAT IS THE PURPOSE OF THIS STUDY?

- We are a team of researchers from [name of organisation]. We want to find out whether the [name of programme] is effective or not, what you learned from it and whether you have benefited from it.

- We also want to know what you liked and disliked about the programme, what aspects had most impact on you and whether there is anything you would change.

- The findings about what worked well and/or what was unhelpful will be presented to [name of organisation] so that they can work to improve the project, and they may also be sent to government departments and other organisations in the same field of work.

WHAT WILL HAPPEN IF I TAKE PART?

- You will be asked to sign our consent form to say that you agree to talk to the researcher.

- We will ask you about how you found the programme, what you enjoyed and achieved, what you found helpful and whether you can suggest any improvements.
- We may also ask you about your past experience as a [type of service user].
- You may be able to tell us a bit about whether the programme helped you or what changes have come about in your life as a result.

WHAT WILL THEY DO WITH WHAT I TELL THEM? WILL IT BE CONFIDENTIAL?

- Yes – we will use what you tell us to help us shape what we write in our report but we won't tell anyone what you personally said.
- We won't use your name in the report and we won't give your details to anyone else.
- Things you tell us about yourself as an individual will be not passed on to your family, teachers, employer or any other agency.
- But – remember that if you tell us that you are in danger or someone is harming or abusing you, or children or young people you know, or that you know that some serious crime is to be committed, we will have to get someone to help you.

WHAT IF I DON'T WANT TO BE INTERVIEWED, OR WANT TO STOP TAKING PART?

- You do not have to take part and you can stop at any time without giving us a reason.
- You don't have to answer any questions you find difficult.
- You will still get exactly the same service from [this programme] and from its workers whether you take part or not.

WHO WILL KNOW WHAT I SAY?

- Only the team of researchers from [name of evaluators] will know what you said. It will help us to see how the needs of service users can be met and how such projects could work better in the future.
- We will take notes of what you tell us but only the research team will see the notes and we will keep them safely.

WHAT WILL HAPPEN TO THE INFORMATION?

- We will use what people tell us in all the interviews, with other information, to write a report about how [name of the programme] is working, how effective it is, whether or not it is of benefit to its users, and how projects like this might do even better in the future.

- There won't be any names in the report but we may want to quote the things you told us.

OK, BUT WHAT IF I WANT TO ASK MORE QUESTIONS OR COMPLAIN ABOUT SOMETHING TO DO WITH YOUR STUDY?

- You can ask us questions while we are here with you.
- Or you can contact [name of evaluators] with a query or complaint. The manager of the study is [name and contact details].

WHAT IF I WANT HELP WITH PROBLEMS OR THINGS THAT COME UP IN THE INTERVIEW?

We suggest you talk to [names and contact details for agencies that might support respondents with any questions or emotional issues raised by the evaluation].

B. A specimen consent form

Consent form

Title of Project or Service being evaluated:
Researcher's name:
Before signing this form, please look through the Information Sheet about this evaluation.
Now please read carefully each point on this form and only sign it if you are happy to consent to take part in this study.

- I agree to take part in the study as described in the Information Sheet.
- I understand that I can stop at any time if I want to without saying why and that it won't make any difference to the support I get from the service.
- The Researcher has explained the study and I have had the chance to ask questions about what will happen.
- I agree that I can be quoted in the report so long as my name or details are not given.

[Include the following statements if appropriate, or delete from your consent form:

- I agree to the interview being audio recorded.
- I agree to the interview being video recorded.]

Signature of respondent: **Date:**

I confirm that I have explained the nature of the Project Evaluation to the respondent, as detailed in the Information Sheet.

Signature of Researcher: **Date:**

C. A format to help you plan your evaluation systematically

Project name:.............................
Our Evaluation Plan
For the period:............................

1. THE PURPOSE OF YOUR EVALUATION

What is the main purpose for which you are evaluating? What questions are you trying to answer? Does the evaluation cover just a particular project or a wider picture of what your organisation does?

2. THE AUDIENCE FOR THE EVALUATION

Who will read the evaluation? How will they use it? Do they have a special focus or particular questions?

3. WHAT INFORMATION DO YOU NEED IN ORDER TO ANSWER THE EVALUATION QUESTIONS? WHAT DO I WISH TO KNOW? INDICATORS – HOW I WILL KNOW IT?

Remember this is certain to require some picture of the 'outcomes' you achieve in the project.

Are there issues of management processes or procedures that should also be evaluated?

How will you show that the users' views were taken into account in the evaluation?

4. SO WHAT DATA WILL YOU GATHER? OR WHAT CURRENT DATA CAN BE USED?

Data required	Method of data collection	Sample (if applicable)	Timetable
(For example) Participants' views of training course	Interviews	20 per cent random sample of students on all courses in 2010	Interviews: Sept–Jan Analysis: Feb & March

5. WHO WILL COLLECT AND ANALYSE THE DATA?

Who will collect each set of data required? Who will analyse each set of data?

6. WRITING UP YOUR FINDINGS

Who will be writing up the results? What is the timetable for the report? What sort of format is needed?

7. IMPLEMENTATION

Who is responsible overall for this evaluation? How and when will you check progress?

Are further resources needed other than current project staffing and finance?

8. COMMUNICATION AND DISSEMINATION

How will the evaluation be communicated and shared?

9. ANY OTHER KEY INFORMATION ABOUT YOUR EVALUATION

Form completed by.................................... **Date**............

D. Suggested headings for an evaluation report

Here we offer some draft content headings for an evaluation report. Subheadings (in bold italics below) will usually be needed below each Section heading. This will offer you a possible structure for your report, depending on what is applicable to your project. Length is a matter of judgement. For some projects receiving modest funding, these headings might be summarised in a short report (4–6 sides) emphasising the evidence of outcomes. Others will need much more substantial reports.

Title page

Title of the project

Title of the evaluation

Period covered by the report (e.g. April 2010–March 2011)

Author(s)

Date of submission or publication

Executive Summary

If it is a long report, the Executive Summary can be used to provide a short overview of the contents. It should cover:

A brief statement of the purpose of the project

Why the evaluation was conducted

The main findings

Conclusions/recommendations/main options for development

Section 1: Introduction and background

Nature of the project, how it is constituted, what area it covers, when it was set up

Particular *needs identified* at that stage

Current aims and targets

Its *users/clients* – Who is it aimed at?

What the project offers – its *activities and interventions*.

Does the project have a particular *rationale or philosophy* behind its work?

The *current inputs* (resources) of the project

Section 2: Methodology

What is *the purpose of the evaluation*?

What are the *specific evaluation questions* it tries to answer?

Who is the *intended audience*?

What was the *evaluation design and methodology*? (e.g. qualitative and or quantitative measures? How were any samples chosen? How was data collected and analysed?)

How were the *views of users* incorporated in the evaluation process?

With the current emphasis on outcomes, how does the evaluation seek to show *evidence for the outcomes* achieved – i.e. what the benefits are to service users?

Section 3: Main findings and discussion of the results

Results on the *outputs* of the project in the period (e.g. attendances, hours delivered, number helped or trained)

Findings – on the *outcomes* of the project (evidence of benefits to users, changes in their behaviour, knowledge, skills, attitudes or condition) and on *management or process issues* (e.g. quality of partnership working, safety procedures, staffing levels)

These findings may include *feedback* from users, their families, stakeholders and staff

Any *patterns or themes emerging* from the findings

Were particular targets met or not?

Relevance of the outcomes *to policy objectives*

Comments, where possible, on the *value for money* offered by the project

[Consider using tables or charts to make the information interesting.]

Section 4: Conclusions, recommendations, options

What *conclusions* can be drawn about the effectiveness of the project?

What main issues or *trends* show up in the findings?

What are the major *strengths and weaknesses*?

Are there particular questions needing *further research*?

Are there *recommendations for future practice*, policy or resources?

How will the evaluation findings be used for *improving the project*?

Are there options to be considered for *future development* or to deal with problems identified?

Useful Websites

Information on the Internet is ephemeral so it is important that you make efforts to find current materials. Some of the most useful sites we have found to date are listed below.

www.ces-vol.org.uk

The Charities Evaluation Service offers free information on evaluation and quality. CES was funded by the Big Lottery Fund to offer the National Outcomes Programme, accessed in the section entitled 'Outcomes online' on this website. Resources include key texts written in 2002–2005, which clarify the terms used in the language of outcomes and indicate a range of means to identify them.

www.evaluationsupportscotland.org.uk

Evaluation Support Scotland has been set up to help voluntary organisations and funders measure the value of what they are doing. The resources section is rich and includes effective links to other sites. ESS present their own Evaluation Support Guides, each comprising 4–6 pages of clear information and examples. To date, there are thirteen offering highly relevant material.

http://managementhelp.org/evaluatn/outcomes.htm

This website offers guidance for planning and implementing an outcomes-based evaluation process, which is entitled a *Basic Guide to Outcomes-Based Evaluation for Nonprofit Organizations with Very Limited Resources*.

www.mandbf.org.uk

The tools section on the Mentoring and Befriending Foundation website has easy-to-use links to resources both from the UK and the USA. The research section lists key findings and links to various evaluations that demonstrate the impact of mentoring. *Impact measurement and evaluation: a guide to effective evaluation* (1999) includes questionnaires designed and used by practitioners, which can be a useful starting point for devising your own.

www.ne-cf.org

This website summarises work on the national evaluation of the Children's Fund. It provides some of the emerging themes, resources and several hundred local evaluation reports. Some of the material is now dated and it does not all address outcome issues but the site offers access to a wide range of evaluation studies on work with children.

www.nya.org.uk

The National Youth Agency provides publications and downloads on work with young people, including some activities suitable for evaluation purposes. The site includes the download for *Capturing the Evidence* (Comfort *et al.* 2006), which is no longer in print elsewhere.

www.philanthropycapital.org

New Philanthropy Capital is a charity that advises funders on how to give more effectively. Research reports on social welfare topics are available free to download. NPC is promoting tools to enable charities to measure their impact. The 'Tools for Charities' section includes a report on the development of a questionnaire to measure children's feelings of wellbeing undertaken with third sector organisations. NPC plans to make this available from October 2009.

www.raguide.org

This site outlines the concepts of Mark Friedman's Results Accountability framework for outcome planning. It provides presentations, tools, exercises and case studies of implementation. www.resultsaccountability.com also offers publications and online papers on the model.

www.surveysystem.com/sdesign.htm

This website offers advice on selecting respondents, the strengths and limitations of interviews and questionnaires and information on designing survey tools. The section on questionnaire design is particularly informative and clearly presented with helpful examples. It includes: question types; rating and agreement scales; question order; layout and how best to present; plus a useful general tips section.

www.uwex.edu/ces/pdande/evaluation/

Guidance and tools on logic models and evaluation from the University of Wisconsin are offered here. There is clear information on the stages of an evaluation, from planning through to presentation, including useful planning charts.

Glossary

Activities: what we do in our projects to achieve the intended purposes and outcomes. Projects can be offering very different activities depending on their aims, their intended audience and their specialist area of work.

Aggregating data: this means adding together the data in our results or otherwise using them for arithmetical calculations, such as averages.

Anonymity: the principle of ensuring that the subject or respondent in a study cannot be identified individually from a report by their name or any other details.

Audience: in this context, the term means any individuals, groups or organisations that will (or should) read an evaluation report or hear about its findings.

Augmentative communication system: any system, such as manual signing or computer-aided artificial speech which aids communication for a person with disabilities who cannot communicate verbally.

Case control study: in such studies the differences are compared between one group that developed a particular form of behaviour or a disease and another group that did not. This enables risk factors for the behaviour or condition to be identified (for example, between offenders and non-offenders or people who develop coronary heart disease and those that do not).

Client or service user: someone who uses services (including a person who pays for a particular service under a contract). In this book, the term is generally used for a person who uses programmes and services provided. Depending on the service context, the term for users of a service will vary and might include pupil, student, patient, tenant, member, participant or simply user.

Closed questions: this type of question is structured to ask the respondent to choose a response from a limited list of options. This could include pre-set categories or choices, points on a scale or providing a specific number, like the number of months on a programme.

Coding: this means allocating a numerical code to particular answers, factors, or themes that appear in words in the data, so that the codes can be entered into a spreadsheet or statistical package for more efficient analysis.

Commissioning: the overall process of deciding what services are needed and engaging providers to deliver them. Commissioning includes deciding the vision for services, analysing needs against existing provision, setting priorities, procurement, and monitoring and evaluating contracts against the outcomes they are intended to deliver. A person who takes responsibility for this commissioning process either on their own or as part of a partnership or trust is termed a 'commissioner'.

Confidentiality: the principle of protecting the interests of respondents by ensuring that information given to the evaluator is not disclosed to anyone else in a way that means it can be traced back to the individual, unless explicit agreement has been given.

Critical incident analysis: respondents are asked to identify and describe specific incidents they experienced which had an important effect on their progress or outcomes (crises, times of major progress, turning points). The accounts and their context are analysed for trends and for what made these times so significant.

Ethical issues: moral concerns about the potential effect of the evaluation. This includes any potentially harmful effects on respondents, service users, the evaluators themselves and the wider society. These concerns lead to practical imperatives for the way in which evaluators engage others in the process. The main ethical principles for research are: informed consent, voluntary involvement, confidentiality, and anonymity.

Evaluation: the process of using monitoring information and other data to make an assessment of how an organisation, programme or project is performing. Evaluation may be *formative* (to improve a project while it is in progress) or *summative* (to sum up achievements at the end of a project or programme). Evaluation may be carried out internally (by the staff of the organisation concerned) or externally (by evaluators from another organisation or by individual free-lance consultants).

Executive Summary: a section at the beginning of a detailed report summarising the main points made in the full text. It should be in straightforward language with enough information for the reader to understand what is in the full report without having to read it all.

Free text comments: comments written by respondents in their own words in response to open questions, not constrained by tick boxes or a limited number of options for answers.

Indicators: are those things you use to judge whether or not you are achieving the right results and making progress towards your outcomes. Indicators are things you can read, see or hear that tell you something about the outcome in question. You devise or select indicators you feel are appropriate to gather evidence for the achievement of your outcomes.

In-kind support: forms of support to a project that are not given in cash, such as the loan of a vehicle, or free use of premises.

Inputs: these are the resources that go in to make the programme work, such as money, time, workers, vehicles or facilities.

Local Area Agreement (LAA): LAAs show the priorities determined by the key partners in a local area that are agreed with central government. LAAs allow some flexibility for local partners to go beyond the National Indicators of performance set by government. A scheme of 'rewards' in the form of Performance Reward Grants operates as an incentive for the local areas to attain above average performance on the targets they set for themselves in these agreements. The government is seeking to simplify LAAs and reduce the number of targets. LAA guidance is revised from year to year.

Measures of ranking: measures which ask the respondent to choose the order or rank in which they would place a range of items or choose a point on a scale closest to their own view.

Median: the median is the mid-point of a range of numbers, values or scores.

Monitoring: the regular and systematic collection and recording of information (in this context, especially of output and outcome data).

Nominal data: categories that simply afford a head count (for example, the category of unemployed people). One item in a category is equivalent to another so that numbers can be totalled or averaged (for instance, the total number of unemployed people or the average number of unemployed). Such categories do not indicate any particular rank order.

Open questions: these questions ask for an answer in the respondent's own words, whether as a word, a phrase or an extended comment.

Ordinal data: these are ranked categories such as 'the most important, second most important, least important' or 'strongly agree' through to 'strongly disagree'. They provide the rank order but do not tell us why the categories are in that order or by how much one rank differs from another.

Outcomes: outcomes are all the changes that result from a programme or an intervention. The term is generally used to mean positive benefits but outcomes also may include negative effects.

Outputs: the tangible products of the project or programme. They are counted to describe and quantify the size of the programme and apply both to activities (for example, number of education sessions offered) and to participants (how many people attended the sessions).

Piloting: a pilot study is a small-scale study carried out before the main research or evaluation to test the methods proposed, and to identify and resolve any problems: a trial run.

Process evaluation: this is an evaluation of the processes involved in delivery of a programme, such as its governance, management structure, staffing requirements and support, planning and targeting, referral systems, or communication.

Procurement: deciding the level of service required, making tenders known, selecting and appointing providers and agreeing the contract.

Quasi-experimental designs: studies designed in this way compare a group that has received an intervention or programme with another group that has not (the control group). Sometimes the group on the programme is matched with the control group on characteristics that are expected to make a difference to the outcomes. This is not strictly 'experimental' in the sense that participants are randomly assigned to receive the intervention or not. It does, however, allow a comparison of the outcomes between those that did experience the intervention and the control group.

Randomised control trials: in such trials, participants are randomly assigned either to a group that receive the programme or to a group that receives no intervention (or a placebo). The differences in results can then be compared.

Reliability: this means the quality of repeatability; if the same data-gathering methods were used by other people on the same group then they should produce the same results. If others can repeat the methods and get the same results, the methods are reliable. If questions mean different things to different people or can be interpreted differently then the data-gathering tools are not reliable. The greater the reliability the more accurately all the evaluation data can be aggregated and compared.

Representative sample: this is a balanced cross-section drawn from the wider population under study so that the individuals chosen share the same characteristics as the whole group. To be representative, samples need to cover all relevant types that are found in the wider group and take these types (such as ethnic groups, ages or sexes) in the same proportion as in the general population. The information from a representative sample will provide a justifiable picture of the whole group with roughly the same results as if the whole population under study had been involved.

Response rate: the percentage of those invited to be involved in the evaluation (ie. those in the sample) that did participate (ie. returned surveys, completed questions or tests). The higher the response rate the more secure are the findings.

Sample: a smaller group drawn from the population under study.

Sampling methods: these are the techniques used to select individuals as subjects or participants for research or evaluation from amongst the wider group under study. (A discussion of different types of samples appears in Chapter 7.)

Service Level Agreement (SLA): An SLA is an agreement between the commissioner and the provider of services. It defines the level of service to be provided under the contract such as the quantity of service to be delivered and the outcomes to be met. It may also set out penalties for failing to meet defined targets.

Statistical significance: the evaluator is often looking for connections in the data and the strength of those connections. Is there a strong connection between the two variables or is it a chance result? (For example, did a particular intervention contribute to a specific outcome?) Tests of statistical significance provide an estimate of the probability that an association between two or more variables is not simply accidental but a genuine link between the variables.

Third Sector: Third Sector organisations (sometimes termed voluntary organisations) are non-governmental agencies which work to further social, environmental or cultural objectives rather than to make a profit. They reinvest any surpluses to further their objectives. They are regarded as key partners to the public and private sectors.

Triangulation: using evidence gathered from different perspectives (from different groups of respondents) or using different methods or measurements in order to increase reliability and validity.

Validity: validity is the extent to which data give a true picture of the subject under study; how far the findings provide a genuine and authentic picture of what is being evaluated.

References

Audit Commission (2007) *Hearts and Minds: Commissioning from the Voluntary Sector.* Wetherby: Audit Commission Publications.

Badham, B. and Wade, H. (2005) *Hear by Right: Setting Standards for the Active Involvement of Young People in Democracy.* (2nd edition, original edition published 2001) Leicester: National Youth Agency.

Bell, J. (1987) *Doing Your Research Project.* Bristol: Open University Press.

Boeck, T. (2009) *Re: action, Youth-led Research: How Youth Action Volunteering Enhances the Social Capital of Young People and their Communities.* Birmingham: Youth Action Network. Available at http://www.youthactionnetwork.org.uk/images/stories/re_action/project_reaction_final_report.pdf, accessed on 08/07/09.

Brand, S. and Price, R. (2000) *The Economic and Social Costs of Crime.* HORS 217. London: Home Office.

British Psychological Society (2006) *Code of Ethics and Conduct.* Leicester: British Psychological Society. Available at www.bps.org.uk/the-society/code-of-conduct/, accessed on 28/05/09.

British Sociological Association (2002) *Statement of Ethical Practice for the British Sociological Association.* Durham: British Sociological Association. Available at www.sociology.org.uk/as4bsoce.pdf or on www.britsoc.co.uk, accessed on 26/05/09.

Brookes, M., Goodall, E. and Heady, L. (2007) *Misspent Youth – The Costs of Truancy and Exclusion.* London: New Philanthropy Capital.

Business Link (2007) *Tendering for Public Contracts.* (4th edition) London: Department of Trade and Industry. Available at www.berr.gov.uk/files/file39469.pdf accessed on 29/04/09.

Centre for Educational Outcomes (2009) *C4EO – What We Offer.* Available at www.c4eo.org.uk/evidence/default/aspx, accessed on 29/04/05.

Centre for Housing Research (2007) *Outcomes Framework for Supporting People – Framework and Guidance for Completing SP Outcomes for Short-Term Services.* St Andrews: Centre for Housing Research, University of St Andrews and Department for Communities and Local Government. Available at www.spkweb.org.uk/subjects/outcomes, accessed on 03/04/09.

Change Support Difference (CSD) Ltd (2009 unpublished) *Heywood Youth Inclusion Project – Impact Assessment.* Leamington Spa: CSD Ltd.

Comfort, H., Merton, B., Payne, M., and Flint, W. (2006) *Capturing the Evidence.* Leicester: National Youth Agency.

Compact (2009) *Commissioning Guidance.* Birmingham: Commission for the Compact.

Cozens, A., Bichard, M., de Groot, L., Digings, L. *et al.* (2007) *Loose Talk and a Hard Nut: Commissioning for Better Outcomes.* London: Solace Foundation Imprint.

Creative Research Systems (2009) *Survey Design.* Petaluma CA: Creative Research Systems. Available at www.surveysystem.com/sdesign.htm, accessed on 06/07/09.

Cresswell, J. and Plano Clark, V. (2007) *Designing and Conducting Mixed Methods Research.* Thousand Oaks, California: Sage.

Cupitt, S. and Ellis, J. (2007) *Your Project and its Outcomes.* London: Charities Evaluation Service. Available at www.ces-vol.org.uk/downloads/yourprojectanditsoutcomes-139-146.pdf, accessed on 03/07/09.

Dartington-i (2006) *Common Language Training Pack: What is an Outcome?* Available at www.commonlanguage.org.uk/pages/lectures/, accessed on 03/06/09.

Denscombe, M. (2002) *Ground Rules for Good Research.* Maidenhead: Open University Press.

Denscombe, M. (2005) *The Good Research Guide.* (2nd edition, original edition published 1998.) Maidenhead: Open University Press.

Department for Children, Schools and Families (2008) *Statutory Guidance on Section 507B Education Act 1996.* London: Department for Children, Schools and Families.

Department for Communities and Local Government (2009) *National Indicators for Local Authorities and Local Authority Partnerships: Updated National Indicator Definitions.* London: Department for Communities and Local Government. Available at www.communities.gov.uk/documents/localgovernment/pdf/11471951.pdf. accessed on 03/04/09.

Department for Education and Skills (2003) *Every Child Matters.* CM5860. Norwich: HMSO.

Department for Education and Skills (2005) *Youth Matters.* Cm 6629. London: Department for Education and Skills.

Department of Health, Department for Education and Employment and Home Office (2000) *Framework for the Assessment of Children in Need and their Families.* London: The Stationery Office. Available at www.dh.gov.uk/en/Publicationsandstatistics/Publications/PublicationsPolicyandGuidance/DH_4008144, accessed on 14/07/09.

Department of Health (2004) *Quality Outcome Framework Final Amended Guidance.* London: Department of Health. Available at www.dh.gov.uk/en/Healthcare/Primarycare/Primarycarecontracting/QOF/DH_4125653, accessed on 04/04/09.

Department of Health (2007) *World Class Commissioning: Vision.* London: Department of Health. Available at www.dh.gov.uk/en/Publicationsandstatistics/Publications/PublicationsPolicyAndGuidance/DH_080956, accessed on 28/04/09.

Department of Health (2009) *Developing the Quality and Outcomes Framework: Proposals for a New, Independent Process.* Consultation paper. London: Department of Health. Available at www.dh.gov.uk/en/Consultations/Responsestoconsultations/DH_096423, accessed on 03/04/09.

Department for Transport (2004) *Guidelines for Evaluating Road Safety Education Interventions.* London: Department for Transport. Available at www.dft.gov.uk/pgr/roadsafety/laguidance/educationinterventions/elinesforevaluatingroads4676.pdf, accessed on 08/04/09.

Department for Work and Pensions and Welsh European Funding Office (2003) *A Practical Guide to Measuring Soft Outcomes and Distance Travelled – Guidance Document.* Methyr Tidfil: WEFO. Available at www.wefo.wales.gov.uk/resource/Soft_Outcomes_Leavers_Study_E7217.pdf, accessed on 03/07/09.

Department for Work and Pensions (2008a) *Raising Expectations and Increasing Support: Reforming Welfare for the Future.* London: The Stationery Office.

Department for Work and Pensions (2008b) *Commissioning Strategy.* Cm 7330. Norwich: The Stationery Office.

Dubourg, R., Hamed. J. and Thorns, J. (2005) *The Economic and Social Costs of Crime against Individuals and Households 2003/4.* Home Office online report 30/05. London: Home Office.

Ellis, J. (2005) *Practical Monitoring and Evaluation: A Guide for Voluntary Organisations.* (2nd edition, original edition published 2002) London: Charities Evaluation Service.

Evaluation Support Scotland (2007) *Evaluation Support Guide 4: Using Visual Approaches to Evaluate your Project.* Available at www.evaluationsupportscotland.org.uk/downloads/SupportGuide4-Jan08.pdf, accessed on 15/07/09.

Evaluation Support Scotland (2009) *Evaluation Support Guide 13: Using Qualitative Information for Evaluation.* Available at www.evaluationsupportscotland.org.uk/downloads/SupportGuide13may09_2.pdf, accessed on 30/07/09.

Field, F. (1999) *The Welfare State – Never Ending Reform.* Available at www.bbc.co.uk/history/british/modern/field_01.shtml, accessed on 27/04/09.

Foddy, W. (1993) *Constructing Questions for Interviews and Questionnaires: Theory and Practice in Social Research.* Cambridge: Cambridge University Press.

Football Foundation and Substance (2008) *Kickz – Monitoring and Evaluation 2008*. London: The Football Foundation. Available at www.footballfoundation.org.uk/our-schemes/kickz/key-documents/, accessed on 30/08/09.

Freud, D. (2007) *Reducing Dependency, Increasing Opportunity: Options for the Future of Welfare to Work*. Norwich: The Stationery Office.

Friedman, M. (2005) *Trying Hard is not Good Enough: How to Produce Measurable Improvements for Customers and Communities*. Victoria, Canada: Trafford Publishing.

Green, J. and South, J. (2006) *Evaluation*. Maidenhead: Open University Press.

Hamblin, A. (1974) *The Evaluation and Control of Training*. Maidenhead: McGraw Hill.

HM Government (2006) *Joint Planning and Commissioning Framework for Children, Young People and Maternity Services*. London: Department for Children, Schools and Families.

HM Treasury (2002) *The Role of the Voluntary and Community Sector in Service Delivery: A Cross-cutting Review*. London: The Stationery Office.

HM Treasury and DCSF (2007) *Aiming High for Young People – a Ten-year Strategy for Positive Activities*. London: HM Treasury.

Hoggarth, L., Anthony, D., Canton, R., Cartwright, I. *et al.* (2009a unpublished) *Staffordshire Fire and Rescue Service – Evaluation of the Crash Course, March 2009*. Leicester: Youth Affairs Unit, De Montfort University.

Hoggarth, L., Boeck, T., Cartwright, I., Comfort, H. *et al.* (2009b) *Doers and Shapers – Young People's Volunteering and Engagement in Public Services. An Evaluation of the Beacon Councils' Positive Youth Engagement Peer Support Programme*. De Montfort University: Leicester. Available at www.nya.org.uk/information/143078/learningandevidence/, accessed on 18/08/09.

Hughes, B. (2009) *Speech to the Local Government Association* Available at www.dcsf.gov.uk/speeches/speech.cfm?SpeechID=898, accessed on 29/04/09.

Information Commissioner's Office (2009) *The Data Protection Act – Your Rights, Responsibilities and Obligations to Data Protection*. Wilmslow, Cheshire: Information Commissioner's Office. Available at www.ico.gov.uk/what_we_cover/data_protection.aspx, accessed 01/06/09.

Kirkpatrick, D. (1959) 'Techniques for evaluating training programmes.' *Journal of the American Society of Training Directors 13*, 3–26.

Lawlor, E., Neitzert, E. and Nicholls, J. (2008) *Measuring Value: A Guide to Social Return on Investment (SROI)*. (2nd edition, original edition published 2007) London: New Economics Foundation.

MacKeith, J., Burns, S., and Graham, K. (2008) *The Outcomes Star: User Guide* (2nd edition, original edition published 2006) London: Homeless Link. Available at www.homelessoutcomes.org.uk/The_Outcomes_Star.aspx, accessed on 15/07/09.

McNamara, C. (1997) *Basic Guide to Outcomes-Based Evaluation for Nonprofit Organizations with Very Limited Resources*. Available at http://managementhelp.org/evaluatn/outcomes.htm, accessed on 11/05/09.

Merton, B. *et al.* (2004) *An Evaluation of the Impact of Youth Work in England*. Research Report 606. Nottingham: Department for Education and Skills.

Merton, B., with Comfort, H. and Payne, M. (2005) *Recognising and Recording the Impact of Youth Work*. Leicester: National Youth Agency.

Munn P. and Drewer, E. (2004) *Using Questionnaires in Small-scale Research: A Beginner's Guide*. Glasgow: The SCRE Centre, University of Glasgow.

National Institute of Adult Continuing Education (2005) *Catching Confidence: The Nature and Role of Confidence – Ways of Developing and Recording Changes in the Learning Context*. Leicester: NIACE.

Neville, C. and Keen, S. (2009) 'Can you put a number on a feeling?' *Giving Insights*. Summer 2009, p.8. Available at www.philanthropycapital.org/downloads/pdf/Giving_Insights_Summer_09.pdf, accessed on 16/07/09.

NHS Information Centre (2008) *Information for World-class Commissioning: The Commissioning Cycle*. Available at www.ic.nhs.uk/commissioning, accessed on 28/04/09.

Office of the Deputy Prime Minister (2004) *Street Games: A Report into Young People's Participation in Sport*. London: Office of the Deputy Prime Minister.

Office of the Third Sector (2006) *Partnership in Public Services: An Action Plan for Third Sector Involvement*. London: HM Government.

Pawson, R. and Tilley, N. (1997) *Realistic Evaluation.* London: Sage Publications.

Penna, R. and Phillips, W. (2005) 'Eight Outcome Models.' *Evaluation Exchange X1*, 2. Harvard Family Research Project. Available at www.hfrp.org/evaluation/the-evaluation-exchange/issue-archive/evaluation-methodology/eight-outcome-models, accessed on 11/05/09.

Rossi, P., Lipsey, M. and Freeman, H. (2004) *Evaluation: A Systematic Approach.* (7th edition, original edition published c. 1972.) Thousand Oaks, California: Sage.

Saleh, M., Anthony, D.M. and Parboteeah, S. (2009) 'The impact of pressure ulcer risk assessment on patient outcomes among hospitalised patients.' *Journal of Clinical Nursing 18*, 1923–1929.

Sherman, L., Gottfredson, D., Mackenzie, D., Eck, J., Reuter, P., and Bushway, S. (1998) *Preventing Crime: What Works, What Doesn't, What's Promising.* Washington: US Department of Justice.

Siegel, S. (1956) *Nonparametric Statistics for the Behavioural Sciences.* Kogakusha: McGraw Hill.

Skinner, A. and Fleming, J. (2007) *Influence through Participation.* London: Improvement and Development Agency (IDeA).

Sloan, J. (2007) 'Rebooting Democracy: Youth Participation in Politics in the UK.' *Parliamentary Affairs 60*, 4, 548–567.

Spicker, P. (2008) *An Introduction to Social Policy.* Aberdeen, Scotland: The Robert Gordon University. Available at www2.rgu.ac.uk/publicpolicy/introduction, accessed on 27/04/09.

Staunton, C. (2008 unpublished) *Evaluation of School Summer Holiday, 2008, Free Swimming Pools Admission: The Impact on Local Anti-Social Behaviour and Youth Offending.* Wirral: Wirral Joint Community Safety Team.

Taylor-Powell, E., Steele, S. and Douglah, M. (1996) *Planning a Program Evaluation.* Madison, Wisconsin: University of Wisconsin. Available at http://learningstore.uwex.edu/pdf/G3658-1.pdf, accessed on 25/05/09.

Tellus2 (2007) *Questionnaire.* London: Ofsted. Available at www.ofsted.gov.uk/content/download/5223/41072/file/Tellus2%20questionnaire%20-%20secondary%20(Word%20format).doc, accessed on 30/04/09.

Times, The (2009) 'Jargon buster.' 23 May, p.25.

Tulloch, S. (1996) *Oxford Complete Wordfinder.* Oxford: Oxford University Press and The Reader's Digest.

Turton, D. (ed) (2006) *Introductory Pack on Funding and Finance – Guide to Procurement and Contracting.* London: Institute of Public Finance/National Council for Voluntary Organisations. Available at www.ncvo-vol.org.uk/uploadedFiles/Sustainable_Funding/Publications/5-_Procurement.pdf, accessed on 05/01/09.

UNICEF (2006) *Every Child Matters: The Five Outcomes and the UNCRC.* Available at www.unicef.org.uk/tz/resources/assets/pdf/join_up_ecm_uncrc.pdf, accessed on 05/04/09.

United Way of America (1996) *Measuring Program Outcomes: A Practical Approach.* Arlington, VA: United Way of America.

University of Leeds (2009) *Guide to the Design of Questionnaires.* Leeds: University of Leeds. Available at http://iss.leeds.ac.uk/info/312/surveys/217/guide_to_the_design_of_questionnaires/1, accessed on 13/07/09.

US Department of Education (2001) *Public Law Print of PL 107–110, the No Child Left Behind Act of 2001.* Available at www.ed.gov/policy/elsec/leg/esea02/index.html, accessed on 05/04/09.

Waterlow, J. (1991) 'A Policy that Protects.' *Professional Nurse 6*, 262–264.

Whiter, R., Plumb, J., Hans, M., and Morris, K. (2006) *Before Signing on the Dotted Line: All You Need to Know about Procuring Public Sector Contracts.* London: National Council for Voluntary Organisations. Available at www.ncvo-vol.org.uk/sites/www.ncvo-vol.org.uk/files/UploadedFiles/Sustainable_Funding/Publications/Procurement_Guide.pdf, accessed on 6/01/10.

Wider Impact Consultancy (2009 unpublished) *Mentoring Referrals and Co-ordination Project: Independent Evaluation.* Birmingham: New Hope Mentoring Programme.

W.K. Kellogg Foundation (2004) *Logic Model Development Guide.* Michigan: W.K. Kellogg Foundation. Available at www.wkkf.org/Pubs/Tools/Evaluation/Pub3669.pdf, accessed on 16/05/09.

Subject Index

Author Index